Letters for Grace

one mother's journey

Jane Nicolet

Acknowledgments

I would like to publicly thank all the authors, thinkers and healers whose ideas helped me recognize that life, even in the midst of crushing chaos, can revive and learn to move again toward something beautiful. Though their words of comfort and thoughtful reflection have been acknowledged throughout the book, those below deserve a special word of thanks:

Anne Lamott's *Traveling Mercies: Some Thoughts on Faith*; John Gunther's *Death Be Not Proud*; Wayne Dyer's *You'll See It When You Believe It* and *The Power of Intention*; Barbara Brown Taylor's *An Altar in the World*; Dr. Catherine Sanders' *How to Survive the Loss of a Child*; and Dr. Joe Dispenza's *Evolve your Brain*.

Thank you. You each touched my life at just the right time.

***

"What the caterpillar calls the end…
the master calls a butterfly."
~Richard Bach

Printed in the United States of America
First Printing, 2013

ISBN: 1492213810

And lo,
I am with you always
Matthew 28:20

For Matthew
April 28, 1970 – September 12, 1998

And to Leslie
whose sweet presence kept me alive
and equal to the fight

Table of Contents

Introduction

To My Readers –

My son, Matthew, died . . . of complications. He was alone, 1100 miles away from me, in a place where I prayed he was finding his brand of peace. By the time he died, Matt had created a life without me and, though he was still at my center, as far as I knew my boy's life barely included his mother. Our estrangement settled my life into an indefinite pause, a quiet circling in measured, reserved steps; his death drew me deeply into thick shadows. Then, when I no longer hoped, he visited my dreams - his energy, standing straight and easily, radiated as would a warm smile. I felt his contentment and my heart released in a sigh. Pause shifted to play and, to its own special rhythm, life began moving forward again.

I first opened to Matt's presence through a package of family photos sent years after his death from far away by his absent stepfather. Snapshots of our celebrations together in a time when love and hope filled my life brought again the utter devastation of bitter loss. It turned my whole being into an achy vigilance – the sort mothers have when they are watchful, concerned about a child's next move. I was fallow ground, waiting for something to shift.

It was then I first allowed Matt into my dreams. "Live," I felt him say. "Just write the damn book." My spirit answered, "OK, Matt, but here's the deal. If I take this on, you have to stick around. I need some answers. Help me - and while you're at it, find me some grace for the journey."

Since that first visit there are times when he wraps a loving arm around my shoulders, when I feel his playful grin just behind me, when I am aware of his keen intellect and calm wisdom guiding my thoughts and words. More often lately I sense his foot in my back, a gentle push into life's next chapter.

I've always been a letter writer; I believe in the shared touch of intimacy delivered through personally-written thoughts that can be handled by both writer and reader. When Matt first left for college, he wrote some wonderful letters home; his sardonic wit and knack for intimate detail transported me into his new adult life. This memory and my own expressive need moved me to choose letters and personal poetry as the vehicle to share my journey since his death. Like joy and grief, the nuances of heart-felt letters and poems are neither fixed nor immutable. They drift to the rhythm of emotions lying close to the surface, helping ideas flow to their own cadence. Within these genres, readers are able to wander with the writer, targeting words, ideas, and images that bring connection to friends and strangers who share meaning.

It has been hard to let others into my grief. Finding easier solace in the inanimate, I turn to books when I'm troubled and finally able to open to the help of other voices. Anne Lamott's <u>Traveling Mercies</u> often speaks to my heart and, in this case, her words provided grace. "It is the unearned love . . . the help you receive when you have no bright ideas left, when you . . . have discovered that your best thinking and most charming charm have failed you. Grace is the light . . . that takes you from that isolated place and puts you with others . . ."   I ached for that light – some bright ideas, so created my own Grace to surface as an ally and friend armed with gentle queries and unconditionally loving reminders, helping to eventually move me beyond my self-imposed isolation, putting me with others and back into the play of life.

This memoir charts the journey of a survivor. My letters to Matt and Grace are the unpacking of my deepest wonderings, my most difficult questions, my search to replace painful, sharp edges with kinder, more loving rounded corners. At its end I longed to experience Rilke's compassionate belief that being patient with our own questions will eventually lead us to unearth and live into their answers. My memoir moves from surviving the first year after the death of a child to beginning the search for answers and respite from grief's inevitable ongoing fallout, considering new possibilities as my mind, heart and soul reach for resurrection and finally recounting some survival truths that sustain me.

Sorrow, my constant companion for the past decade, has acted as my greatest catalyst. A bruising need to use its trauma pushes me to make meaning of chaos, to somehow produce. My life became a kind of search and rescue mission, with me playing both roles. The nearing of my mother's death brought Matt's loss back to me in fresh and complex ways and I knew the time had come to actually complete my saga, moving forward somehow to bring an end to the "damn book."

As I sit here composing, my mind settles on the truth of Tim O'Brien's words in <u>The Things They Carried.</u> Our stated enemies were different but simply being at war with anything allows the warriors to share some common truths. O'Brien's words resonate deeply: "In any war story, but especially a true one, it's difficult to separate what happened from what seemed to happen. . . . The pictures get jumbled; you tend to miss a lot. . . . when you go to tell about it, there is always that surreal seemingness, which makes the story seem untrue, but which in fact represents the hard and exact truth as it *seemed*."

So here I am, sharing my hard and exact truth - the shaping of one mother's life since Death, disguised as a sad and uncomfortable policewoman, knocked loudly at my front door. *Letters for Grace* is my walk in bereavement - what I forced grief to teach me about survival, and what I allowed my son to share about love, hope and forgiveness.

Part One: It Begins with an Ending

September 12, 1998 – September, 1999

And So It Begins . . .

I didn't hear the doorbell.
BC's urgent voice, his face close to mine,
finally rouses me to fear's unsettling presence.

We sit close together, my 3:00 am visitor and I,
knees almost touching.
Miserable eyes watch me; hands grope for mine
while a gentle voice delivers hell's most intimate life sentence.
I grasp for balance, my eyes reading the truth in hers.

Finally, the details,
the ritualized phrases crack open my world and I rise,
willing her gone,
my limits for pain long since breeched.

It's dawning.
Dry-eyed, I lay in my husband's arms until isolation's siren
call is stronger than resistance.
On my own, curled in a chair,
I wrap myself tightly in the blankness of my next chapter,
making mental lists
while the new skin of pain begins its fold around my heart.

I had a son named Matthew who was alive yesterday;
I lay my heart in his hands on the day he was born,
believing we were meant to step together to life's intricate,
        lovely music.
But his hands have fallen open and I shift.
Death takes the lead
in a new, tangled dance.

Matthew Christopher:
18 letters spill over the first line
certifying new life,
identifying the spirit and energy of love
in tender human form.
Tiny, waving fists brush exposed heart;
an audacious yawn and unblinking gaze
leave me no choice:
leaning down so our foreheads touch
I breathe in and seal you into me.

September, 1998

My darling boy,

I see you for the last time in a pine box. It fit you and our purpose. Your dad, sister and I decided you would prefer cremation – little fuss, moral, courageous, straightforward; we wanted to honor the way you accepted the world and your place in it.

You are dressed in clothes that suit you but that I never touched or had the chance to choose, a painful reminder that we have been separated. I was not the one to go to your closet and select your favorites. I admit to feeling desolate – an outsider in this place and time of your death. Yet, surprisingly I am not repelled by the looks of you, lying alone and contained in this strange place. You are still my boy – now well taken care of by thoughtful strangers.

We are alone, you and I, as I say my goodbye privately. Are you here, in this room with me? I believe your spirit may have already flown, though I ache to feel it close. Am I just too sad, too guilty to sense any presence beyond your lifeless form in front of me? In life, your fierce energy and bright spirit seemed perpetual forces propelling you forward into your next philosophical conversation or another imaginative idea more easily sold by your winning smile. Now Death leaves us both motionless.

My hands fist tightly; nails digging into my palms in an effort to – what: Feel? Hurt myself? Hold on? I don't know and am beyond caring. I wonder if you watch me take my Venetian cross and place it across your hands. I can almost hear your gently chiding tone, "Mom, that piece of jewelry is for the living. I don't need it." Well, Son, here is my truth – I need to crawl into that box with you, but can't. So, that cross is me, my heart and soul. Though it was bought in the midst of joy, laughter, and hope, its job now is to take my place in the fire with you.

I've missed you for so long and the inescapable reality that I will never wrap my arms around you again shocks me like a blow. The breath I have been holding for two years, waiting for your full return into my life, escapes. How can I stand it?
Mom

October, 1998
Dear Grace,

How interesting it is that you've chosen now to come back into my life. Thank you for your kind note and sympathy card.   Yes, it was so much more than a surprise.   Having a 3:00 am visit from the police with such a message will live on as my nightmare. It is kind of you to want to help.

Both memorial services are complete – one on the coast where he was living and one here at his Colorado home.   While in Oregon to collect his body and few possessions, we - Matt's dad, sister and I - decided to have him cremated. We planned and then held a brief service for people I had never met but who shared his life here and seemed to care deeply for him. Then we drove to the coast and scattered half of his ashes in the Pacific. The second service, so much more difficult with extended family and dear friends, happened later when most could get to Colorado. Then about eighteen of us, the immediate family, drove into the Rocky Mountains and scattered the remainder of his ashes at a spot on the rocks where he and his sister often played. I could never bear to leave him in the ground. I am so glad that his dad and sister agreed to let him fly free in death; in life his failing body made such freedom difficult. Now he can move unfettered and I'm grateful.

Back at work, I find myself sleepwalking through the steps of buying the new house, pending before Matt's death. BC needs this change; I sense it strongly. We will be moving soon and the thought of packing is mind-numbing. I wonder where that energy will come from. BC assures me this move will be a blessing in disguise, something to take my mind off my son.

Again, thank you for reconnecting. It has been years since we've talked. Please don't think you need to keep up with me right now. I expect we will have some time to visit when I get my feet under me again.

Jane

November, 1998

Grace,

You always were persistent when you thought you knew best about something. And as I remember you mostly did – know best, that is. So, after your last note and taking some time to actually digest your kind offer to help by simply listening - to my disbelief or anger or pathetic cries - I accept.

Though I am robotic most of my waking moments, when I quiet myself to think or process or simply be present, I find I have things to say. Questions, anger, and disbelief scream in my head whenever I allow it. Still, having things to say and actually saying them aloud are two different things. I sit in grief which masquerades as everyday life. The hole is too deep to find my way out, so what may pass as words or thoughts to others are really me shouting upwards, wondering if I'm heard – or even coherent.

Should you really want to accept my ravings, I fear they will bring you letters full of hopelessness and bitterness. I am surprised at the ugliness of my thoughts. In any event, I give you total permission to burn any or all of them, or simply never open them. I expect they will be my stretching, my reaching for ways to understand the unthinkable, to stay somehow connected to the living. I could so easily stop life now; sound dramatic? I am beginning to accept it as my new normal.

If the craziness of this mother in grief proves to be more than a friendship can endure, you have my total permission to ask for some sanity for yourself – some space from me. I promise to honor what you need.

Jane

December, 1998

Grace,

I received your birthday note a few days ago. The world continues to spin, though it doesn't seem right that I get older and Matt can't. Thank you for remembering. All three of us in Matt's family - mother, father and sister - have birthdays in November. It was impossible to do the act of celebrating anything so we didn't.

We are in the new house. BC and I are keeping busy getting this huge house transformed into a home. Flooring, painting, new furniture to fill rooms, plans for a future in this new space he seems to already love. I am exhausted but continue to work full time and sleep little. I am told by those who watch me perform this wretched life schedule that it is time to slow down and rest, but rest brings quiet, and with quiet comes the time to think and remember.

I am looking ahead to Christmas and wondering how to get through it. Our growing blended family has shared lots of wonderful times together during this holiday. It is painful to think about the changes we will be making now – even more strange to imagine doing things the same. I am torn. How do I help others be at ease, act a good guest, be a graceful hostess while trying to stay upright? What is my role in this new skin? How many *shoulds* will I hear, how many will I heed?

Do you remember that dog that we found curled up under the lilac bush at home? I think we were about twelve, taking a walk around the outskirts of the yard. She looked so pitiful – fur matted and eyes so sad. When we described it to Mom she said the dog was there "licking her wounds." We found that so weird – going off alone to hide, feel pain or fear or any emotion by yourself. And really, can you lick something and make it well? We couldn't fathom that at all then.

One of my bigger wounds I wish I could reach with the swipe of a healing tongue is close to the surface and so tender. The last time Matt and I said good bye was two years before his death. Believing we would still have hundreds of times to greet and part from one another, I paid little special attention to this good bye, shared in a flurry of family celebration. The guilt of not being able to construct a mind picture of our last hug, his last smile formed just for me, my last touch of his face tears at me. When you're a mom paying attention is rule number one isn't it? Like the dog of our childhood, I only want to hide, to find an isolated space to live in my own ugliness.

Please don't worry about me. In fact, don't think of me at all until another note comes to you. If I believe you are, I will have to find a way to help you feel better and I don't want to be responsible for that. It's the space I'm in – a mother with empty arms.

December, 1998

My son,

I miss you in this world. Were you aware when your dad and I cleaned out your room right after you died? Were you there? Did you watch my face when I walked in to your bare room? Imagine, I thought, his entire life in one room. It gave me a shock, noting what must have been important to you, those few things you kept in this space. Unopened cards and packages from your family, last year's un-cashed Christmas checks, the family watch your dad gave you years earlier, lots of books and school papers, a few pairs of jeans, some underwear, shirts, socks – you had always lived in your mind and this room proved that. Things were never your thing, were they? Ideas - now that was your thing. What ideas lived in your head as you created this space in which you died?

I never knew if you listened to my phone messages or opened my notes or packages, or if you were planning to call me or set a time to come home for a visit. As I look around at what remains, it becomes painfully clear I will never know. I can no longer dream about the times you and I will laugh and talk together again. Reality is only silence, no hope you will respond when I tell you I love you.

I am bereft. What could I have done to change the outcome of your life story? What did I miss? What did you need to hear that I never said? Did you know that I loved you beyond reason every day of your life? Did my daily prayers, begging God for your return, for a call to share how you were feeling, for any indication you might be ready to talk about our last few years apart, ever reach you? I need to know; the bewilderment and anger eats at me daily. Do you watch us from your new place? I allow my broken imagination and whatever fractured hope still left to create a sunny, gentle place for you using my conjured concept of a heaven. I need to believe you are now in the ranks of the angels, an energy with the ability to interact with everything, anytime and anywhere.

Matt, I swear if one more person tells me that "life goes on" or that your death was "meant to be," I won't be responsible for my bad behavior. What I know is death goes on, and on, and on . . . . You are ever in my mind, cherished and loved, just as you were when you were in this world. Though a part of me knows better, I still wait for your call.

Mom

Don't observe yourself too closely.
Don't be too quick to draw conclusions from
what happens to you; simply let it happen.
Otherwise, it will be too easy for you to look
with blame at your past, which naturally has a
share in everything that now meets you.
Rainer Maria Rilke

January 1, 1999

Good morning Son,

I woke up today and looked out our most marvelous picture window. Truly, it is what makes this bedroom one of the best spaces in our new home. The sky fills it, and dotted on the far horizon are the shapes and colors of the old town area that you loved. Perfect way to open a new year - Yes? I wish it were so. My reality doesn't extend into this wonderful view for long; it meets a dark wall as soon as I remember you are no longer in this world with me.

I remember you as a fine writer. Did you journal regularly? I have never been able to get into that habit even though I, too, write. It has been interesting; some friends think that journaling will help me and continue to talk to me about it as a way to promote healing. So, I bought one: Sarah Ban Breathnach's The Simple Abundance Journal of Gratitude. It combines journaling with contemplation of all those things for which we are to feel grateful. Admittedly this is a stretch for me right now, but somehow I think you are proud of me for trying.

It is within reaching distance, on the bedside table. I expect I should try to begin and end my day with positive, grateful thoughts, and so I will. But, sweetheart, do you find irony in this exercise - finding gratitude in the midst of grief? I do. In the first part of the journal the author lists 150 often overlooked blessings for me to consider. Right up there in the top 26 is "holding your child in your arms." Another high on the list is "the health of those you love."   As I hope you have always known, neither of those blessings did I ever take for granted or overlook; the power of their truth in my present is overwhelming. Still, for those whom I love still with me, I'll try to find delight and hope in living by recalling wonderful things. Maybe someday, while persevering in gratitude, I will even get to number 82, finding myself "letting go gracefully without regrets." Today, this is inconceivable.

Your stepfather is stirring next to me and I don't want him to wake into a new year with worry. The more engaged I stay in something, the easier he seems to feel. So, I am picking up the new journal to move my thoughts away from where you are to where I must stay for now – in a world with those who need me strong.

January 1: this entry opens to possibilities through this quote by Melody Beattie: "Gratitude unlocks the fullness of life. It turns what we have into enough, and more. It turns denial into acceptance, chaos to order,

confusion to clarity. . . Gratitude makes sense of our past
. . ." So, I will begin my lists with some hope that these
words may hold truth.
Mom

February, 1999
My good friend,

Your Christmas wishes were so dear. BC and I
decided to spend time differently during this first
Christmas without Matthew. We stayed in town just long
enough to get our remaining children together once and
headed for Illinois to be with extended family. Breaking
the old pattern was a lifesaver for me. I could not face
spending this Christmas trying to recreate what I used to
love so much. Odd that it took me so long to realize that,
as a parent, I wrapped the trappings of holidays in
packages for my children; without their responses to
them, all the carefully crafted plans mean little.

Thank you for sticking with me. Finding time for
you, to continue to talk through the ongoing sanctity and
abhorrence that is reality, helps keep me sane.
Jane

March, 1999
Dear Grace,

I've been busy trying to get some answers, which
seems the only way to stop my downward spiral into
places that are both welcoming and scary. I decided to
get cerebral, an attempt to bring some kind of order to the

chaos of the unbelievable, to move into the reality of other thinkers, to establish a reality of my own that doesn't hurt when I breathe. My study just brings more questions, but at least it gives me a purpose and calms my restlessness.

I started by reading Kubler-Ross and at the same time asking myself why I choose a book centered on responses of those who face their own death since my death is not the imminent issue at hand. The author's words resonate deeply with me now: grief, regardless of its center, is universal and presents in everyone through inexorable mixtures of feelings and behaviors. Since you mentioned her work to me earlier I know you're familiar with those well-advertised five stages of grief. I must admit I have only given them an academic nod until recently. I think I am in many stages at once; the chaos in my mind gives me a tendency to get really angry at a moment's notice. I don't think I even acknowledged the Bargaining phase. Since Matt was already gone, the timing was off and there was no opportunity to offer my own life instead. Though I longed for it, I couldn't rest in Denial; the farther out from his death, the more acute my pain became. I longed for a buffer to the inevitable ugliness that memory brings. I think I tried to barrel through it in order to reach other stages that are supposed to help me tame my grieving – fast. Patience and allowing the natural unfolding of things have never been my strong suits. Words for Jane to live by: In grief, there is no control.

I am unable to stay in bed, to be quiet in one place, to sit still. Though I am really only performing, sleepwalking through daily activities, I persist. I am terrified to allow the actuality of *it* (sometimes I can't name *"it"* aloud) to rest in and on me. I continue to perform the part of a whole person at work and at home. Just yesterday a co-worker met me in the hall at school, solicitation so evident in his face. All I could do was simply smile, shake my head, hold up my hand, palm toward him, turn and walk away. When I isolate myself in order not to hear or see the pain in others, it allows me to continue to keep my own pain locked away. Death haunts me, but I have to keep standing tall to survive.

My study tells me that this inability to rest in the reality of it all will cause me problems sooner or later but honestly, Grace, I just cannot stop running. The sound of the demon behind me is so terrifying.

Jane

March, 1999

My son,

Last week I composed a letter for Grace and then, as I read some of my own musings, I was acutely reminded of the parallels between how I am behaving in response to your death and how you behaved after that fateful, final blood test confirmed the fear-filled sentence of your Ankylosing Spondylitis diagnosis. Who learned from whom how to be artful in isolation – to go inward, learn and plan on your own? As the parent, I accept the responsibility but, my beautiful Matt, you developed into a master.

During the latter years, after you moved to Oregon leaving me physically and emotionally behind, I no longer knew how much, or even if, you loved me. I longed to know. Not communicating with you ate away at me and our relationship. You were a pragmatist. I understood that to deal with the pain and limitations of the disease you were carving out physical and personal boundaries for your own life journey. But to hold on to an *us*, I had to believe that in time those boundaries would be more inclusive of those you left in Colorado.

Over time, our relationship became a memory – an emptying vessel held together by passionate hope. I believed without a doubt you would find a freeing absolution within your personal quest, forgive yourself for not being the perfect son, and forgive me for not saying, being, doing whatever would have kept you closer and more comfortable in my company. I trusted that the memories of what we had and were together would eventually return you into the arms of my unconditional love.

You died first. Hope died with you.

Your mom

March, 1999

Matt,

Your birthday is coming too soon. Anticipating it is unsettling. Gazing into the mirror, I see your mother's pinched face – that look of pain creases in familiar ways now. I cry for you when I'm alone. What will I do when April comes? How will I ease the pain of your grandmother when she ties the celebration of her own April birthday to yours, just a day apart? How will I help your sister so that she has the space and support she needs to remember you without worrying about me or your dad during the saddest time of our common life together?

I think I am beginning to perfect my daily performances; they are becoming second nature. I want to show that your mom can handle things just fine. I think it best if others don't have to concern themselves with me, don't spend much time thinking about me at all. I abhor the thought of being in a spotlight. If they aren't concerned, they'll leave me alone and let me trudge through another day without you.

Then again, why do I care what others think? Why do I continue to put one foot in front of the other? I hate to think about April. It scares me. I miss you in this world and love you beyond breathing.

Mom

April, 1999

Dear Grace,

It is Matt's birthday month. How can that be – so soon! I am afraid of what this month will bring; how will I handle the pain that a simple calendar turn brings. I've spent some time thinking about the *right way* to grieve during this time. What should I do during the actual day? Is it best to go to work or to stay home? And if I stay home, will wandering around the house or cleaning or watching TV or reading or staying in bed help anything? Pretending to be fine at work really is a lost cause for me on many days and I can't imagine making that work on Matt's birth date. The word *endure* continues to pop into my head, but that word only makes me angry. Why? And, really, what does it mean in this case? Just stay alive? If it weren't for Leslie and BC I don't know what I'd do. Endure? Doubtful.

Living through this month drags me deeper into memory so I suppose it's as good a time as any to share how the arrangements unfolded – was it only seven months ago? Matt's dad, his wife and I traveled by car to Oregon to do what those who are left do. Matt was living and working in Oregon and we needed to clean out his one-room space, create a service for his friends there, make arrangements for his body, and bring him home. Our trek was long and uncomfortable; we stopped for the night in Utah. I remember being really light-headed as I stood outside the motel room, breathing in the mountain air, feeling a brisk September wind and watching a slash of clouds catch the setting sun. Any other time I might have found this beautiful; now I felt only tenuous and unbalanced. I retreated to the stark motel room and made the decision to write to our son. I took pencil in hand and on some motel stationary, tried to say goodbye to my first-born. The words came easily, tears even more easily, but sleep stayed away.

I don't remember who read it at the service the following evening where his Oregon friends gathered to say goodbye, but I do remember being glad that I did it. I made a copy and it was read again, along with a letter written by his dad, at his second memorial service in the town where he grew up. If you want, you could read it sometime; I have put it away in the space that holds most of what is left of Matt's things. I don't open the door to that space now, but realize I will need to do that sometime. When I do I'll read those words that were my tribute to him.

I still have the blue suit that I wore to that first memorial, as well as the black dress that I wore to the second. I know I will wear them both again; I can't bear to part with either. On special occasions I will take one or the other from the closet and wrap us both in it. I image that wearing it year after year will remind me that grief is always in fashion.

Jane

April 28, 1999

Darling Matt,

Your sister, young niece, and I planted a crabapple tree in your memory today, your birthday. We went to the nursery and found one that we thought would please you. It flowers with sweet pink blooms in the spring (sadly, it occurs to me that I don't know if you even cared about blooms), and has berries that the birds can feed from during the winter (now this I know you like!). This tree is for all of us. Both Leslie and I want something we can see and touch when we think of you – something we can watch grow and develop throughout the years. I need to watch live symbols of you interact within my world. Through this living tree you are now a part of my world at home.

Did you remember that your niece's birthday is just five days before yours? I am sorry that you never knew her very well; she knows you through family stories and pictures. She calls you Uncle Matt and looks hard at her mom and me when we speak your name. Though only three, your neice has some of your sensitivities. She feels our deepening sorrow and continues to look for evidence of it as we talk and work in the yard. It is as if she, too, is an old soul living the life of one much younger. It saddens me that you only held her a few times, and weren't around to listen to her delightful babblings and laughter, dry her tears, or watch the sister you love so dearly operate as mother. She is very good at it, which I know is no surprise to you. Was it too painful, somehow inconvenient, or was there just too little time for you to grow close to your sister's child? What was I missing? Did you need something you couldn't ask me for?

Anyway, it was good to get my hands dirty and to smile at your sister with a sweaty rather than tearful face. My muscles feel the strain of doing something new and worthwhile. Moving a living thing into the ground so we could exchange love and beauty for emptiness made me feel better. I believe you would be proud of us.

You are still my beating heart – my very breath.

Mom

May, 1999

Grace,

The school year is winding down. I have rolled into a pattern of work and weekends that is familiar and keeps the most acute pain at bay, though I don't feel very well physically. I guess that is to be expected. I simply continue to listen for the alarm each morning, move to its demand, and put one foot in front of the other as I go through the days.

You were right when you told me how important friends will become. I have two or three dear women who are always present even before I know I need them. They are, quite simply, lifelines for a drowning woman who continues to carefully put on makeup. So, when I got this last call I was unprepared . . . and the next shoe dropped. (I am convinced that fate, death, or whatever it is that destroys the complacency of calm has many more than two shoes to drop.)

I had an interesting and dreadful conversation with an acquaintance who works with BC. She is no stranger to the pain and loss of death, so when she called for a coffee date, I was looking forward to a no-explanation type of girlfriend talk. She got to the point of our visit by sharing how concerned she was about BC; his behavior at work is different and he appears sad and distracted. She never actually said "Jane, get your act together," but that is what I ended up saying to myself. I certainly didn't want to be responsible for my beloved being more strained or distressed by my grief journey. I need to do something differently.

Still, and maybe I am being unfair, I must admit I got a bit defensive. What was I supposed to do? Wasn't everyone's job just to keep me wrapped in as much cotton wool as I needed? Whose child is dead? Whose pain is greater than mine? How am I supposed to somehow rise to the occasion of helping others too? And, really, why wouldn't he be sad and distracted! Is his behavior out of character or somehow odd; is there something else I should know or worry about?

At any rate, her words made me stop and take stock of my behavior. Guilt, now my most familiar friend, jumped forward to help: I am being selfish. I am suffering too much in front of those I love, causing them to suffer even more because they care for me. Right then I decided to change how I expressed my grief. I am going to try to use the times away from others to go into those darkest of places. When I am with BC, I will lift the mood, move ahead and show that I can heal with the best of them.

This is a part of the journey that I didn't expect to travel – I had no idea that guilt and concern came in so many varieties, required so much energy. I continue to feel exhausted no matter what time of day. Something has to change – what must I do to balance my inside darkness with the outside façade I keep trying to perfect?
Jane

May, 1999
Grace,

What a quick reply! Your comments about me perfecting my isolation skills as I grieve are noted. Thanks for your concern. But since I am using your compassionate presence to balance a very unsteady me, you get to hear the reality no matter how ridiculous or ugly or whatever. That was the deal – right? What I know is that isolation continues to be my truest companion. It expects nothing from me and its lack of need provides my only breathing space. During isolation I am myself, unvarnished and true, as I walk this hell called daily living.

I need to be more upbeat at home. I cry in the car going to and from work but when I get home I am really working at being more conversational, interested in BC's work and just generally doing life in ways I pray appear more normal.

I refuse to be selfish, imposing my grief on others. Really, who wants to hear that you're feeling breakable to the touch? Hopefully, if I pretend to be among the living long enough, it will become true.
Jane

June, 1999
Matt,

Summertime is here in its full-on beauty. Showers, sun, and our incredibly blue skies build our days. Was this season your favorite? I always thought you loved summer best. When you were little I remember having to push you out the door, away from the television, into the arms of fresh air and active friends. You went slowly until you discovered it wasn't so bad. Then you fell in love with the freedom and speed of riding; I don't remember exactly when it happened, but sometime in high school your bicycle took center stage.

Yesterday NPR was reporting on the Tour de France. Did you follow that race as a young man? Could you enjoy the passion and success of others when you could no longer ride without pain or fear?   It never fails: whenever this time of year rolls around and the race details begin to take over the airways, you are on my mind. I so often feel guilt for being a part of the genetic cocktail that kept you from being the cyclist you might have been. I loved seeing your face after a ride, red, sweaty, literally glowing with the pleasure of possessing a body that was able to work and play hard. Instead of smiling at the image of you in your riding gear, jumping on your bike in preparation for a ride, I feel immense sadness. I so much wanted that joy for you.

When you could no longer ride because of the pain in your hips and back or the very real fear of how debilitating a fall could be for you, I cried. I hope you never knew that. As I sit here writing to you, I can honestly say I wish that we had talked about your diagnosis and all its many ramifications. Why didn't I tell you that your pain was mine? I know you understood that simple fact, but we never said the words. Instead you went away. I am left to wonder if you decided not to come back to me because we couldn't admit our pain to each other.

So, here I am crying again when what I want is to remember you with joy. You were the first person in my life who I loved utterly, without reservation. My heart is more open and vulnerable and I am a different person because you were in my life.

I am going to try to stay away from you, your memories, for a little while this next month. Your stepfather and I are doing our summer getaway. We are off to Florida soon. I hope to rekindle the ease and simplicity of leisure we shared before your death. You were such a wonderful, accepting, and playful pragmatist (though that description seems like an oxymoron, you actually made it work!); I could use your advice about how to behave during this time. So, as always, wish you were here.

I love you,

Mom

July, 1999

Dear Grace,

Summer has a new shape to it. We have been working hard for months on the new house and so are treating ourselves to a short trip to Florida. I have, quite simply, adored our travels together. That time was always an oasis in the midst of our busy lives, filled with time to laugh, relax and reconnect. I find myself begging fate or whatever to grant me a gift - that this trip will hold some of the old feelings of lightness and joy I remember.

These last months have been so hard. My health - physical, spiritual, and emotional - is on a consistent downturn. What I have always been able to count on is gone. I hurt in new places; I cry easily; food holds no interest; anger smolders right below the surface – all the time. All of these are new entities in my life. I want to rail at . . . who? Who turned my world on its side? What can I blame? Hopefully this latest round of doctor visits will glean some answers for the physical issues plaguing me.

BC and I walk a fine line, trying to interpret what each other means by our words and glances, smiles and frowns. Our communication is strained in ways that surprise me. I always thought we were moving to the same rhythms of life, could almost read each other's minds. He hates watching me change so profoundly. I don't know how to navigate the days' steps so he can more easily walk this horrid journey with me. I still feel as if I have to hide my real self from him so that we can proceed with life as usual. How can I do that when usual is gone forever? And the bigger question I have no answer for: how many more mornings can I wake and slip into survival mode?

I am afraid to tell BC or anyone how I really am after ten months on this journey. The world in which I find myself is an ugly one; no one, especially the ones I want to protect, deserves to spend time in it. Once again I am going to bury what I can. If I believe I can again be normal long enough I am convinced it will come true. (I know – I can see you smiling as you contemplate the whole "normal" comment.)

Still, I refuse to let anything get in the way of our happiness during our time away. We so need this time to begin to repair a togetherness that is slipping away. I don't know if I am more afraid to tell and show him what I really feel, or of what will happen to me and us if I continue to play this life charade.

Don't expect to hear from me. I am on vacation from Death; I want to experience life again this summer. Keep your fingers crossed that I choose the right roller coaster seat to ride the season out.

Jane

> Grief can't be shared.
> Everyone carries it alone, his own burden, his own way.
> *Anne Morrow Lindberg*

August, 1999

Grace,

Just a quick note to answer your letter. No, Florida and time away were not an answer for us. He was distracted and so I worried about him. I think we were both trying to recreate an experience whose time has passed. I will never be the same; I think that scares BC. He liked things the way they were before Matt died and doesn't seem to know how to cope with a wife he no longer understands. What I am discovering is I need him to cope, to communicate with me in new ways, to tell me that we are together in this and will be ok in time. I feel like a failure but am too low to do anything about it. School starts too soon. I am already tired.

Jane

September, 1999

Grace,

It has been a year this week. I feel his loss like I imagine a gaping exit wound would feel. This first, like his birthday month, will mark a pattern for me for the rest of my life. I am prepared for that; I have accepted it, yet I don't know what such an acceptance will mean to the shaping of my life. Do I have the power to shape it? Frankly, now I don't. I feel like so much flotsam, riding the waves, trying to keep my swollen, wobbly head above the water. The returning thought that plagues me still is that my son died alone, without my loving arms around him or my voice soothing his fear. Will I ever emerge from this nightmare?

I am living the truth that when someone dies without you as a witness, imagination can run absolutely amuck. Because of my fear of the answers, I could only ask those questions I hoped would bring both truth and kindnesses – the easy questions, based in factual boundaries delivered by experienced responders. The Coroner, the local police, the funeral home director, a best friend, all who knew I needed gentleness more than air itself gave me answers that kept me alive. He didn't suffer; he was unconscious near the end; he went quietly; he loved us; he knew we loved him; he was happy and was enjoying the life he had made.

The ticks of days, months and years have been spent considering what those last hours were like for Matt. Having no way to know with certainty, I long for the best, searching for peace while imagining the very worst. BC tries so hard to take my mind from the pictures that I continue to paint for myself. Poor man - I believe that facing my awful fears, even tentatively, may be the only thing that will help me move beyond them. Then, of course, he has to live it this way as well. I'm certain he wants me to do things differently. I don't know how. I am simply surviving and these horrid pictures are a part of it all. Times when I am not engaged in some sort of organized work or play I wallow in this self-imposed hell of wondering. Telling myself it will pass and I will find peace is as often believed as it is bitterly denied.

Yet I know I have much: a husband who loves me and will walk this journey with me and a daughter who deserves my strength and needs me alive. All this helps me decide to get up again tomorrow.

September 1999
Son,

How to describe you to someone who never knew you as a boy, a young man: A spring ready to let loose – to bounce up and forward into a project; a shy, thoughtful soul, watching others, deciding if they would accept you, love you, be worth your energy; a loving, indefatigable attitude; a quicksilver wit; an amazing intellect; an infectious sense of humor, rarely filtered by social niceties; a wisdom far beyond your years; or just as a blue-eyed, curly headed blonde boy with a playful, earnest smile and an eagerness to please. You were all those things and so much more.

As you grew it was as if the wisdom of an old soul looked through your young eyes. Your open, expressive face could register pleasure, reticence, mischief and surprise at a moment's notice. As you grew in knowledge, understanding, and pain, you learned masterfully to mask all that you felt. I feel guilt when I think of your mask. How could I have helped you guard against its need or shed it once it became a part of you?

What could I have done to prepare you to feel more secure and more able to share your worries, joys and pain without fear? Questions like these rule my life.

Do you remember when your sister, you and I moved clothes from our home into the condo on Silverthorne? Your dad and I were splitting up; I was moving out and leaving the three of you in our family home. It was a Sunday evening and darkening skies made me feel even lonelier, aching with guilt and sadness at what was happening to us all. I was talking calmly, thanking you both for helping me, and making pathetic attempts at normalcy, hoping to help you and Leslie feel less awkward about our brokenness. You spoke up from the back seat in a kind, calm tone. I don't remember the exact words but I recall them indicating that you understood it was time for me to go and were surprised I had stayed for so long. You were thirteen and instead of flinging teenaged angst at me, you gave compassion. You gave me what I needed to be able to get through that evening – and beyond.

Honey, when they ask me to describe you, I will tell them you were wise and kind well beyond your years with a heart and soul, both large and beautiful. And then I will tell them I miss you beyond words and that the world needs forgiveness because you are gone and I remain.

Mom

Yes, I know

Yes,
I know.
You want to help,
to wrap me in wise words,
healing arms,
ideas both profound and hopeful
that will shift my path toward light.

You're sure you understand.
After all, you've been battered too.
You remember a mother,
taken before you were ready,
a favorite cousin or dear friend
lost just recently.
You remember the experience of unreasoning fear and
dreadful pain -
You've lived the meaning of unbearable.

You need me present with you;
my words, rational,
my laugh, genuine.
You'll feel better if a flicker of hope moves in my eyes,
and I come armed with the extinguisher
to lessen grief's fire that extends between
and singes us both.

Yes,
I know, but I can't help you help me.

Part Two:
What do you know . . . Hell looks just like another day

Fall 1999 – Fall 2001

Alone,
do you recognize what's happening?
Is there a curling of fear,
a clutch of shock?

Alone,
do you call for help,
try to reach out . . .
or just breathe it in?
Do the walls close in
or melt into nothingness,
welcoming in a rush of freedom?

Alone,
is it warm,
peaceful, as you drift toward the
outskirts of what you've touched
into what you've professed?

Alone,
do you decide to ride the wave,
believe the loose ends will finally knit together,
intellectualize
and mark the passing of your own life?

Alone,
I have no balance;
I weep, wondering what happened,
despairing that you may still be
alone.

"The fear of the unknown is behind us . . .
we have already taken a long look at hell."
Sarnoff-Schiff, The Bereaved Parent

Fall, 1999

Dear Matt,

It has been just over a year. I suppose I should be thankful that I can actually ask these questions and be brave enough to listen for the real answers. I have been afraid to even consider the answers even though I did ask the coroner all those months ago about the basics of your death and accepted his soothing tone and answers as balm. But now I go to you: Did you suffer? Were you afraid? Did you feel alone and abandoned? I know that I could have done nothing but bring fear and torment to the room, simply take up space, be present with you as you passed, but the fact that you died alone without me close absolutely haunts me.

I have so many questions: Were you afraid? Did you actually intellectualize it all as you experienced the event? Did your years of study, philosophy and living with painful acceptance make a difference? Were you intrigued, even prepared, to move beyond us all? Did you think of us, those who love you so much? Did you understand that we wanted to be with you no matter what? Is it possible you were grateful to do it without us?

I'm sitting on your new bench, downtown on the library lawn, an area we both loved, thinking about all the questions whose answers terrify me. I think you would like it, this well-crafted bench; in fact, I see your smile at its placement. It came about because we needed a tangible place to visit you. Instead of a grave site which would never have suited you anyway, your dad, sister and I decided to have a commemorative bench built and placed close to the city library. We had a memorial plate affixed into the back of the bench: "What the caterpillar calls the end, the Master calls a butterfly " This Richard Bach quote becomes my mantra, and a vibrant, free-flying butterfly my symbol of an ever-alive you.

So here I rest, and ache with my need to have you beside me. The air is crisp, a green blanket of October grass spreads in front of me, and from your beautiful, sturdy bench I watch children skip toward the front door of a place you loved to be. It's a good spot to watch the energy of living unfold, but I can't smile or turn my thoughts beyond my unyielding need to know. Did you suffer, son? Did you know I loved you more at your ending than I could have ever believed possible at our beginning? I am afraid, but I will listen for your answers and pray that I can survive them.

Mom

Winter, 1999

Dear Grace,

The month of family birthdays and giving thanks is upon me. I appreciate your card; it came early again this year; I must be on your mind. Your consistency reminds me I am real and not the lonely phantom I often feel. Really, I understand that I am never actually alone, but most of those I love – Matt's grandmother, father, sister, stepbrothers, uncle and aunt - are dealing with his death in their own unique ways so it feels as if our lives are fragmented, each of us alone even in our togetherness. As usual, I try to stand stoically within the storm of it all – a space I haunt rather than own. So, when you quietly and consistently show up in my life, it reminds me that I and the experiences I'm living are very real.

As I live through this season of the year it occurs to me that how I am able to handle this ongoing heartache hinges on what I believe about myself, as well as death and life. I am starting to understand a few things about me that impact my ability to live through Matt's death over and over again. I'm not sure I trust or even think very highly of the *me* I invented all those years ago. Still, I am beginning to understand that what I have come to believe and how I live out those beliefs shape my grieving.

I read somewhere that life is lived forward but understood backward. I must admit to you, dear Grace, I loathe the idea of looking back; it is unbelievably painful to consider the beloved people and things that have flowed through and beyond my life. I long to hold on to joyful times with those I love. I despise changes that I haven't initiated. Growing older, losing friends and family only makes me want to hold on more tightly to what I have. I detest it, but living has a pace all its own and has never heeded my controlling hand. I cannot even put into words the depth of my fear as I consider such lack of personal control. Keep looking ahead, I warn myself.

All in Matt's immediate family have a November birthday; tough celebrating life right now, but each of us tries in our own way to allow the others to celebrate us. BC is huge into birthday festivities. It wasn't until we were together that I even counted that day as special, just another day, more of a period, marking an ending to the list of special times in November - Matt's dad and sister, Thanksgiving and then, as November winds down, my birthday. Number four in a string of observances – enough already!

Long story short, for years I tried to create a space where no one would feel obligated to make a big deal of my birthday. I thought it was a bother to grin and bear one more "big day." (Yes, Grace, I hear your question about what that long-held belief says about my own self concept.) But my exuberant husband just does not allow that; he makes me feel as if I deserve royal treatment simply because I am alive and in his life. It touches me and I have grown to be thankful for this new way of looking at being celebrated by others. That is one of BC's biggest gifts to me.

I think he has another pampering plan in place this year. I want so much to show loving appreciation for his gifts – want him to know how lucky I feel that he is in my life. I pray my smile and embrace will feel sincere to this person who is trying so hard to glue all my broken pieces back together. I am obsessed with nurturing what I have; fear of anyone else I love leaving me is an ever-present, weighty burden.

The two of us are off again to Illinois and extended family for the Christmas break. Though I realize I'm taking BC away from his children and grandchildren whom I also miss when we're gone, I don't seem able to face a Colorado family Christmas yet. I count on BC's forgiveness for this selfishness, in the same way I trust that Leslie and her dad will care for each other during this upcoming, dreaded season. I cannot bear to honor a holiday in the same place where I last saw my son alive. I will be strong for Mother and other kind family members who will watch me for signs of sadness and, if I can control it, see none.

I know your presence will be a blessing in the lives of those with whom you spend the holiday season, just as you have become a blessing in mine.

Jane

Winter, 2000

Dear Grace,

A new year! We made it. Y2K and all its potential bedlam have become simply another example of Faulkner's "sound and fury" indicating nothing beyond our own fears. Why do new opportunities and situations bring humans such concern? We certainly know how to forecast the worst. I wonder what I should be learning from jumping into a new millennium with more ease than expected.

We are in the second semester of the school year. I think it was Emerson who said "the first wealth is health." An accurate statement that reminds me of where I feel most impoverished right now. I cannot seem to get well. I continue to make the round of doctor visits, seeing both new and familiar ones, a traditional and alternative mix and match – looking for answers that will help me sleep, enjoy and digest food, and begin to make some sense of the various unusual aches and overwhelming tiredness. My body is a burden, and my spirit, were it a color, is surely a dull grey.

Please, let me apologize; it seems as if I never say anything positive on my side of our communications. I feel the need to stand up straighter so that you will believe I am on the way to being just fine. Consider it said!

Jane

Winter, 2000
Dear Grace,

My cocoon of isolation is receding like the swelling around a wound. My grief feels exposed to the air, the sunlight, the reality of all around me. It seems I am beginning a new stage in this awe-filled and awful journey. These days are now marked by worry and suffering of a whole new genre. Sleepless nights are still plentiful and always committed to worry about the daughter who is still alive, the husband I must be neglecting, the flagging faith that is supposed to uphold me, and the alternating fragile or angry thoughts a strong, healthy person should somehow endure with more understanding and fewer fears.

I have trained myself over the years to believe I can do anything if I simply will it and remain strong, so of course gave myself the assignment of becoming the very model of "how to do grief." My normal days are about displaying false smiles, laughter during inane, unimportant conversations, invoking my son's name as often as I can stand interjecting it, battling memories and valiantly trying, at all costs, to keep the blackness of my grief to myself. Still isolating for some protection, I am becoming more open to the needs of the world around me, especially BC and Leslie's. The blanket of sleepwalking is unraveling, forcing me to become aware of the temperatures outside. This new awakening to feeling introduces me to another level of hell.

Memories flood my senses to the point of drowning. Rarely do I spend a day without crying. My eyes always feel grainy. The pictures that I insisted remain displayed through the house have me meeting Matt face to face daily. I relive our lives, interconnected from his birth to his death. In his early years, before the diagnosis of Ankolosing Spondilytis the summer of his high school graduation, Matt was a golden child. Loving and loved, he sped through life with a powerful intelligence, an open heart and a quick, endearing wit. Parenting him spoiled me and I fell into a rhythm of taking for granted that he would always be the sunshine of my years. Now I battle the ever-present demons of guilt and obsessive worry. Every time a phone rings I am certain Leslie is hurt, in trouble, and needs me immediately. I worry about her death, which I know I could not survive. I lean heavily on just a few people who can only guess at how bad things are because I only let them part-way into my own personal house of horror.

This journey is not kind to God or religion. Born in the traditions of ritual and common life, my understanding and beliefs about prayer, faith and God's place in my present chaos are tenuous. Forgiveness is only a concept I remember acknowledging in passive acceptance; it remains a real concept, but now there is nothing passive regarding my feelings connecting forgiveness and God. How could an omnipotent God allow life to flow out of my boy – a kind, gentle, loving spirit who graciously brought joy and service to others? How dare this God take my son before we had found our way back to each other! Didn't we at least deserve a heads up? How can I believe in, let alone forgive, an all-powerful God when I've never felt assured that my prayer, faithfully delivered daily, sending Matt unconditional love, was heard? I am overwhelmed with a fury I can't express. Inside me sits a ball of searing anger; heat and sparks surely singe others who come close. My body and mind never rest. Forgiveness is not an option, neither for God nor me.

This is one of those letters you should burn before reading – (I must remember to write that on the envelope). If you do read it, please don't bother to answer. I plan to lose myself in school, shutting the door to other realities as tightly as I can. I think only putting one foot in front of the other and riding the wave of structured work can serve me right now.

Jane

Winter, 2000

Hello Son,

Here I am again spending a second Illinois Christmas holiday without you but close to your grandmother, uncle, and aunt. Oh how they adored you, and still do.

BC and I watch your grandmother closely. She was the one person I most worried about actually telling about your death; I made sure your uncle was with her when I had to say the words. I suppose I didn't trust that she would survive it. Now, two years later, she is pale, a little tentative as she watches me for signs of sadness, but not frail. Her strength amazes me. Your grandmother is my role model for this latest walk through hell, just as she was my most gentle and loving unconditional supporter when I rocked the family by leaving your dad. Her faith in God and the inevitability of goodness and grace throughout all things are astonishing to one who now questions everything.

I say I make the trek back to my family roots to support and strengthen the ties to those far away. What I am beginning to understand is that it is they who hold me up. I return to them because no place else gives me any comfort. I will not say this aloud to my Colorado immediate family – wonderful children and grandchildren - who consistently surround me in loving ways, so I lay it at your feet instead. I can more quietly find you in my roots and I let them nurture me in ways no one else is allowed to do. We repeat holiday traditions, eat together, laugh lightly and watch each other while we miss you. It's awkward but real and I feel fortunate that I am enfolded in something so rooted.

Living through Christmas Eve is the most difficult for me. My memories of you, your sister and step-brothers joining BC and me in our cozy little home are so very dear. There was so much laughter: Finding enough standing room in the kitchen to visit while we all cook and clean up together; choosing who would play this year's Santa; watching your stepfather first open, put on and then dance around in his yearly underwear gift; taking turns talking about memorable moments of our week; and attending a church service together. I had lovingly created this ritual time that served to warm and solidify us as a family. Now Christmas Eve is a time to forget; I am trying to rebuild it as a space to nurture your grandmother and remind your uncle and aunt that I appreciate their love for all of us who grieve. When it isn't close and I can think of it objectively, this holiday is an occasion to serve the needs and hopes of others.

Objectivity is not a strong suit now – perhaps next year. Anything is possible I'm told.

Everyone sends their love,
Mom

Spring, 2000

Grace,

Thank you for your calls. I have had my head down while my feet move me through the days. Your indications of ongoing care were appreciated even if I never acknowledged them. Trust doesn't come easily to me right now, but I am learning to trust that you are with me in this hellacious journey for the long haul. When things are at their most tentative, you still seem close – it comforts me enough to actually move my back away from the door and squint into the dark, and once in a while even notice a glimmer of light.

You asked me once before Matt died, "What do you do when really bad stuff happens?" I remember being pretty glib and easily spouting ideas that I believed and thought I would always practice. After all, I had already lost my father, experienced a divorce that made me question my own sanity, and survived the fallout of an aching estrangement from my own children. Surely I understood loss and its fallout.

But now I can tell you what I really do when the inconceivable happens; I return to old patterns – those behaviors and interactions that are familiar, comfortable. I simply try a do-over. I depend on my ability to control the situation. (If I am really paying attention, I hear a shadow of laughter from beyond when I say *control*. I, of course, shrug it off.) After all, and you know this better than any other, I always strive to take charge. If I can make certain there are no surprises in this chaotic circus I call my life, I can keep all the balls in the air. Juggling is not so bad when all the balls are the same shape and size and when new, sticky and misshapen ones aren't tossed into the mix.

The most vile ball of all bounces around me daily now and, though this grief ball brings an anxious energy with it, I continue to try to balance it equally with the others and tell any who ask: "Thanks, but no, really, I think I've got it. I'll let you know if I need anything." "Hold on tight," I tell myself. "You know what to expect. Just do it, get up, one foot in front of the other, keep the hands moving, the balls in the air."

Life continues what it does so well - flows forward in paths independent of my permission. And, finally, I have had to listen to its demands. Death, the physical end of things precious, visits me in both small and profound ways, and much to my distaste, reality's ground rules aren't fixed. So, I admit it: I have no control over the caprices of this circus called life. It moves to a beat of its own.

I'll contact you when I can.

 Jane

Spring, 2000

Grace,

Just a quick note - finally, something positive, interesting to report. An acquaintance at the local university asked me to join his teaching staff. It seems he thinks I have some skills that would easily transfer into the higher education realm. BC and I have talked and I think I am going to say yes to the offer. The position starts in the fall and I find it both exciting and nerve-racking. It is change, but the rhythm of my personal life is in such flux that shaking up my professional life might actually bring an odd kind of balance. My teaching friends at school have been a nurturing force in my life. It is a risk to leave them and the cocoon we've created together. Though a little daunting, I do think this opportunity has come at an important time. I need good chaos for a change.

Speaking of good chaos, BC and I are talking about returning to Europe. We toured Italy with the chorale the summer before Matthew's death. Another musical tour, this time to France, is being planned for next June. We are both a little tenuous about the memories it might bring, and BC worries if he should spend so much time away from work, but we are talking our way through it as a possibility. I am really proud of myself; it is a big step, opening myself to the memories this trip is bound to bring. Still, I really want to do it for my husband; he loves traveling, and this trip would be an opportunity for us to create new memories together. I'll let you know what we decide.

Can you believe how much this note talks about life rather than death? Am I finally doing more than surviving? Do I dare say that life, at this moment in time, holds hope?

Fingers crossed -

Jane

Spring, 2000

Son,

As you may be noticing, I am a mess! I decided to tell you about it instead of complain one more time to those who actually inhabit the same planet I do. The doctor contingency I visit must be relieved I pay for the continuing privilege to involve them in my ongoing litany of aches and pain. We all keep trying new remedies to bring me back to physical health. My most rational self knows that I will move beyond this - whatever it is, but I am not always in touch with that part of me. Right now I spend a lot of time searching for a balance within this new environment where a desperate, unhappy human called your mother re-learns the newest rules for survival. Your stepfather is hanging in with me, though I feel his frustration more as the months pass. The more I work to make a change, the harder it is to wake up the next day with the same complaints.

The best part of now is some excitement I feel about a trip I'm anticipating. Two close friends have talked me into a girlfriend trip to New York City for July 4th. You may best remember these two wonderful women as those who sat on the living room floor with me, talking about you as we packed boxes. Your funeral was a week earlier. I was trying to control the panic I felt leaving a house I loved and walking through yet another big loss. The three of us were filling boxes with books for the move into a new house – me, in tears, and they, gently helping me move through the motions. I still see the love in their faces and it warms me.

Anyway, the three of us are going to fly into NYC, see the sights, go to a couple of plays and watch the fireworks. BC likes that I'm on my way to something different and fun. It will be my first time on my own (without him) since your death. I can't blame him for wanting some time away from a wife who is no longer the same person he married. I am hoping this trip will do us both some good, maybe even actually bring us closer together as we realize how important we are to each other. Somehow we have to rebuild a new life with one less child to hug.

Mom

Summer, 2000

Dear Grace,

We never did spend much time talking about your trip to New York City, did we? Saying this aloud reminds me how self-absorbed I have been, more so now than ever, I'm afraid. Maybe the next time we talk we could spend a little time sharing those things we both enjoyed about our individual trips.

Traveling without BC was a first for me – our many trips were always filled with the kind of laughter that comes when people easily read each other's thoughts and anticipate the joy of the other's reaction to situations. BC and I have that synchronicity so, of course, I wanted to bring him into my trip as fully as I could. And, though I relished seeing a new place with dear friends, I missed my husband, not only his presence but also the ways he would have expressed his own joy in this trip.

However, sharing anything with him turned out to be difficult. Though I called him every day, only once did I actually talk with him. I admit it was really disconcerting to have lost so much contact with him – the tentative me needs the stability of him. Of course, because I am still in the headspace of continual worry my thoughts turned to the surety that something horrid had happened to him: He was sick, had been in an accident, had decided to finally run away from home, you know, all those places a fragile mind goes when fear trumps every other option. He did return one of my earlier calls and I was relieved to know all was well at home. Still, and I hate saying it aloud, even to you who now seem to read my mind and heart, BC was distant. His voice and words were cool and tight with reserve. They sent me into that stomach-sinking kind of panic that stayed with me throughout the trip. I continued to call home daily, leaving messages of missing and loving him while working to keep from affecting my friends' enjoyment with my own anxieties.

When I got home BC made it clear to me that he had not missed the *me* I have become. He believes I have changed so much that we are no longer the same couple, the same people, who began our relationship. Well, I don't think I handled it at all well. I actually felt anger – of course I'm not the same person and never will be again! I asked that he also think about how he is handling his grief, and wondered why he couldn't see the strides I was making in being more available to life and us. I was stunned. When did all this doubt about the reality of us together happen? Where have I been?

Tough conversation and one I could only partially absorb, only partially believe; it was so unexpected. BC is talking about his unhappiness, and evidently he talked with others about how to handle it all while I was gone. With their counsel he decided that we can keep trying to work through the chaos delivered to us by death. Although this could turn into a nightmare, I just can't believe that we won't survive together. He knows I struggle on life's shifting sand and he wouldn't abandon me to navigate it all alone. We have loved each other too well and too long to not find the common strength to see our way into a future. That belief is what is holding me together. I can't talk about it anymore. When I think back on the conversation, fear dispels any ground I thought I had gained.

Jane

"There is an uneasy time when belief has begun to slip . . . when the consciousness is disturbed but not yet altered. It is the most dangerous, important, and ongoing experience of life. The beginning of change is the moment of Doubt. It is that crucial moment when I renew my humanity or become a lie. Doubt requires more courage than conviction does, and more energy; because conviction is a resting place and Doubt is infinite –it is a passionate exercise."
John Patrick Shanley

Fall, 2000

Dear one,

Summer is turning into fall, the season of school. I have such a keen memory of you going off on your Oregon State University exchange student adventure. You worked hard to make the transfer from CSU to OSU a reality so I knew it meant a lot to you. I was worried for you, was happy for you, and was making tentative plans for how to visit and keep you close to me, but it was your dad who drove you out to the coast. As I sit composing this letter to you I wonder where I was. Do you remember how that all came about – your dad getting the honor of that most important rite of passage for you?

I wonder if it would have made a difference to our communication, or lack of it over the ensuing years if I had somehow forced my way into that trip. It turned out to be your final move from your hometown. You took on the role of visitor for the rest of your life. I know you were aware of how tentative I was with your dad. I still carried the guilt of leaving you all and I didn't believe I had a right to be fully vested into all the important family situations. It took me years figuring out who I was with you and your sister after the divorce; I was still tentative about my place when you drove away to make your way in a world apart from me. I wish one of my memories of us all was sharing that rite-of-passage trip, and I ache because I have no such memory and have to take the responsibility for that lack.

Did I just stand by even though I wanted to jump in? Did my guilt once again get in the way at a crucial time? Would it have made any difference to you? To our relationship? Would it have embarrassed you if I had insisted that BC and I follow you and your dad on that trip out? These are questions I ask you, knowing full well I can only guess at the answers.

The photos of you as you unpacked and stood in front of your newest home at OSU were of a young man, happy and ready for a challenge. You were standing straight, your body not yet bent by disease, and your smile delighted, not yet reserved. I know from early letters that you reveled in the experiences created in your new lifestyle. Later, as the disease progressed, life got harder and more painful for you. Letters stopped, and I could almost physically feel you pulling away.

If you were here now, son, I would invite you for coffee or a beer and ask you to talk with me about this time in your life. Through those last few years of your life when you were totally out of contact, I prayed for and really believed that we would have such a time together; you would come back to me and our relationship would mirror what it once was – a mother and son who laughed together, talked philosophy, knew and shared unconditional love.

But you aren't here and to survive I must discover a way to untangle my heart from grief's intricate, ever-present bonds; otherwise, I feel I may be lost. Because I wasn't brave enough to assert my love in those earlier days, did I lose you even before I had to?

Your mom

Winter, 2000

Grace,

My new job at the university is going well. It brings new challenges as well as additional work so it, plus continuing to work through the renovations on our new home, gives me plenty of reasons not to think too much. I work, eat and talk about the day with BC, sleep a bit, and start the whole cycle over the next day.

Though our life together has taken on a different texture, less nurturing and more fragile, BC and I still move through our days together. Because I am still trying to mask my ongoing sadness when we're together, I feel as if I am more active and alive in our conversations. A good friend once said to me: "If you pretend long enough, it will become true." Feeling "normal" is now a pretense; in time I expect it to be my new normal. I want to save a marriage I love to a person

I love, so am prepared to do what is necessary to make that happen.

The writer in me searches for words to describe how I feel I and my life are interacting. I've unwittingly been detoured onto a roller coaster - one on which I'm tied, hands and feet; one that is gathering speed and moving me farther from a husband who is planted on solid ground, seemingly apart from my ride. There are days when I feel we are a strong, loving couple who want nothing more than to be in love and contented with life. Then there are the days of twists and turns, ups and stomach-dropping downs that remind me of the impermanence of everything I still hold dear.

After dinner last week BC told me that no matter what I might hear from other people, he is not having an affair but is totally faithful to me. I blink awake with those words and try to take in what he means by them; of course he is faithful because ours has always been a loving relationship built on solid ground. He has always called me the love of his life, told me we must never leave each other but talk through problems, never allowing them to pull us apart. So, of course, I told him I believed in his faithfulness. And I do, without a doubt. I know that we can build, can be strong again, and even though the life we knew and loved would not be the life of our future, I want to believe it can be beautiful. His face shows me this concept is not his reality.

My world experiences yet another tremor. Grace, is it possible for me to try harder? To be stronger, better, more worthy of our life together?   Somehow I must manage this roller coaster, untangle the knots that fear and pain use to tie me onboard. I am so weary of thinking and analyzing it all.   My latest challenges, being a support system for Leslie, performing through holidays and family observances, and achieving balance in the chaos of what must appear to be everyday decision making to others, are my agenda. No more talking about it, just doing.

I am moving into the season of working harder at saving my marriage and with it, the only life I can conceive of having.

Jane

"The only sadnesses that are dangerous and unhealthy are the ones that we carry around in public in order to drown them out with the noise; like diseases that are treated superficially and foolishly they just withdraw and after a short interval break out again all the more terribly; and gather inside us and are life, are life that is unlived, rejected, lost, life that we can die of."

Rainer Maria Rilke

Spring, 2001

My son,

Have you been watching me these past months? Sometimes when I am teaching my classes, working with college-aged students, I imagine what it would be like to have you as my student.   I consider how I present something, or the way I ask a question, or the discussions I facilitate and wonder - would Matt like to be sitting in this room with me, learning and sharing this unique experience with his mom? Would you acknowledge our relationship or would we go through the semester at arm's length?

This professional change is a breath of new life. I relish the challenge working at the university presents. I use its gifts to hide from you. Confusing, right? On one hand, I wonder what you would think; at the same time, I long for you to stay out of my thoughts. Grief is tricky, crazy-making business. It has been a little helpful for your stepfather as well; he doesn't seem as compelled to drag us into ideas or places that are more comfortable for him. I am busy in a new way, so life nuances slightly. We share pieces of our common living more often, with less intensity, and I must smile more because I fear his disapproval less. We are still tenuous with each other, tiptoeing through the minefields of needs and desires that used to be so familiar and comfortable. Yep, grief is indeed a tricky bastard.

I am so relieved that BC has said yes to the Europe trip. And, hooray, I am finally feeling physically more like myself, so my energy level will match his. I am genuinely excited; I mean, really, how many times does one get to sing in Notre Dame at a Sunday morning mass? Our touring and singing schedule is amazing, but I sense a reticence in BC that surprises me. He does so love to travel and clearly enjoys new experiences with friends, so I'm confused. You remember him that way don't you?   Charismatic and always ready for new adventures while demanding the best outcome in every encounter - remember?

I find myself counting on this time away from what has become our normal stressful life to become that new adventure, that best outcome, that experience to launch us into our next level of relationship. We need this time away from your memory because I believe that space might, strangely enough, bring us closer to you and each other. I am after making new memories and then discovering how to wrap them lovingly around those we keep of you.

Mom

Summer, 2001

Dear Grace,

Good to hear you finally received all four postcards. We were able to visit and perform in such astonishing places. My sense of history, art, music, and beauty was steeped throughout this trip. I believe I gained physical and emotional strength throughout our time in Europe. Though I cried periodically, remembering Matt as I sang my way through a beautiful musical repertoire in amazing venues, for the first time those tears were more healing than destructive. Surrounded by friends who simply and quietly acknowledged my pain allowed me to move within grief in a healthier way than I have so far. It was a gift, those days in Europe.

Unfortunately, BC and I made memories, but not the healing ones I prayed for. We spent some wonderful time together and I was reminded of the kind of loving travel partners we have always been, but he was uncharacteristically sick during part of the trip, and other times simply distant. We haven't really dissected the trip together yet. As pictures come back, I hope we'll talk about it and I will get a stronger sense of how he feels about the trip. My latest plan is to continue being upbeat, no matter the circumstances. I am putting all thoughts of loss on hold. I know that sounds as if I am back at controlling, and I am; BC - our relationship - needs me, and to save what I have, what is lost has to take a back seat.

Jane

Summer, 2001

Dear Son,

Something has happened that I think you would love. I have a chance to go on a mission trip, working for a long weekend helping with housing projects at a Native American community in New Mexico. I remember so fondly your passion for social justice and helping to save, well - everything. What a kind heart, gentle soul, and imaginative mind you brought to this earth. I am poorer in so many ways without you, but I must not concentrate on that now.

Anyway, I jumped at the chance to be a part of this mission trip and thought about how you might want to go along if you could. Though your stepfather is not as enthusiastic as I, he is willing and so we will be driving to New Mexico in a few weeks. Actually, next month's trip coincides with the time of your passing – almost three years to the day. Living through this dreadful anniversary doing something for others might just be the perfect way to face it. Another reason I want to take the long drive southwest to the reservation is to spend some quiet, alone time with your stepdad. I know you've noticed: we need time and space from everyday life to process our life circumstances, our choices, and plan our next steps.

Time is a precious resource isn't it? I plan to use this opportunity to remind both BC and myself that I still have the ability to love and give to others. Still, I can't seem to shake my confusion about his lack of enthusiasm for our mission opportunity and it only serves as a reminder of the importance of our being alone for a while – we have lost touch with each other's moods and needs. My days of taking our relationship for granted ended this summer. And though I'm almost afraid to voice this hope aloud for fear of jinxing it, I am optimistic and excited about the possibility of another beginning.

Your loving mom

September 11, 2001
Matt,

Can you help me understand the core of fear and anger that must be present to cause today's violent devastation – the horrific terrorist attack our country has suffered? You're in a place filled with love and acceptance, right? Do we humans have to experience our own death to finally get a wider, more inclusive view of the humanity with whom we share this planet? The anniversary of your death is tomorrow. I hate that I may always remember your passing with the same mind I remember the senseless death of thousands of others on our east coast.

I will listen for the wisdom of the angel I believe you have become. Help me stay balanced on this tightrope that stretches over the chaos of shock and death. I am thankful that your step-father and I leave on the mission trip next weekend; his reaction to this tragedy confuses me. When I called just to hear his voice, to brush up against a connection borne of love, his voiced words seemed dismissive, annoyed. Clearly I was bothering him instead of loving him. I pray we will lose ourselves in caring for and thinking of others and a new connection will be born.

Mom

Fall, 2001

Dear Grace,

My world has been torn from its axis again. Yes, 9/11 is chaos personified and its horror folds over every event in all our lives right now. Still it is with apology to any who are experiencing first-hand this huge personal tragedy, that I say the terror I feel now trumps all else in my world. The mission trip I had such high hopes for began with BC sharing a letter with me. Before we even reached the state line, a personal list of disappointments and needs, written by my husband and presented to me, dictated our hours of conversation.

I tried staying open as we talked through his letter, a missive filled with how I continued to fail the relationship. By the time we reached the reservation I was exhausted and confused. We made it through the weekend without much more discussion, just doing our best individually to complete the work and interact with others on the trip. My terror at losing another person I love coupled with something I ate combined to make me as sick as I have ever been. By the time we got home I could only go to bed. Two days later, several pounds lighter, I emerged to limp back to work and to begin a new chapter, one in which I watched my marriage crumble.

We're talking about what's next. I am asking for counseling. We'll see. Hope wanes and the black hole of this new reality opens wide.
Jane

Fall, 2001
Grace,

I woke this morning with the sure knowledge that my husband is headed out the door. He can no longer stand being in the same house with the grieving me. He's moving out. I can feel your question – no, he didn't say those words but he has been hinting at it since he presented me with the letter last month and I felt something break away this morning. He was dressed for work and I was lying in bed watching him get ready to leave. I don't remember the exact words but they cut through any last shreds of my well-developed denial.

I held myself together until he left the house. It was still early and the sky, dark. The life I have been living, already so fragile, is dissolving. I remember smirking at the melodrama of women who, in movies, threw themselves on beds and wept loudly. I joined that melodrama this morning. My grief feels inconsolable and not the least melodramatic.

He's talking about "time apart," and mentions a mutual friend with whom he'll stay for a while. I will inhabit this large house alone – the same house that he so badly wanted only three years ago. I will come home after work to a dark place, eating and drinking by myself, eventually sleeping in our wide bed alone, all the while wrapped ever more tightly in those same thoughts I have been running from for years.

Jane

Fall, 2001

Matt,

I know that you already know this, but I have to write it out as a reminder of my reality: your step-father left me today – really left me. Have you sensed, seen my panic over the last weeks? Damn September – my god, how I hate this most beautiful of months. October is shaping up as its equal.

Pretend long enough and it all comes true – right? Panic morphs to single-minded pretense, all in the hope that he will come to his senses, remind himself of all I have been through, of all we have been to each other over the past 16 years, and be able to look ahead to creating a life after grief. I begged the gods to move him so that he wouldn't, couldn't, add to my pain by leaving. Surely he still loves me too much for that kind of betrayal. He will sit down with me, call me his sweetheart, take me into his arms and tell me we are going to work it all out.

He has wanted to get away from me for weeks; I think I represent death to him – yours, his and mine, ours together. I can tell he was hoping I would say words that could make his leaving understandable – that I wanted him gone or I wanted to be alone. But I couldn't do that; it would be untrue. Our familiar connection was holding all my separate pieces together while I healed from losing you. I was so very careful to not talk about you, to continue to put him, and not your loss, in the center of my world. I really believed that if I pretended long enough to feel whole and beautiful for him, he would stay and our life would knit itself back together - I would be whole again and we would be stronger for it.

Are you surprised? Does his leaving affirm something about him or us you knew? Will he be back? Does he just need time on his own? Son, at this moment I feel more alone and afraid than when you left me. Then

I had him to lean on. I want to appear strong for your sister so now I'm on my own, unbound, falling into wide open space, a kind of darkness, a void.

Mom

Fall, 2001

Dear friend,

Yes to most all your questions: I am eating, but still losing weight. I am drinking; for some reason BC comes to the house before I return from work and opens wine for me when he checks in on the house and cat, so I have this inexhaustible supply ready and waiting. Could that mean he misses being with me, continues to care from a distance? It causes me to hold hope. Sleep is intermittent; the television my mindless company.

I did go to see Mother and the Illinois family during both holidays. The train was more soothing and slower than flying; you were right about that. I used the extra time to prepare myself for telling the family about losing another part of our circle. Though I kept it from Mother during Thanksgiving – just couldn't bear to hurt her at such a deep level again so soon – I used Christmas to bring everyone into my reality as it now stands. The telling is done but the tears are ongoing. I did call a professional therapist and will meet with her as the new year begins. I have a shred of hope that BC will come with me; we had always promised each other we would never leave the marriage without time in counseling.

However, to your one question: No. I don't feel "incredibly betrayed" by my husband. Frankly, I don't know how to label or even access such a negative feeling about someone who has been an intimate and loving part of me for so many years. It's just easier to blame myself for the reality that death, grief and loneliness are permanent residences within our relationship.

Our combined children express a gamut of emotions – surprise, sadness, anger; our friends are in various stages of disbelief. He quotes statistics to me. Though I don't remember specifics, I do know he seems to be taking a kind of blameless comfort in the large number of marriages that disintegrate after a child dies. A convenient rationale for our eventual demise, I suppose. I take comfort from none of it.

I have to go now. Its dark out, I'm tired from it all and I just want to lie down.

Jane

The door closes. . .
behind us,
finally.
Locked shut, no key in sight,
it defines desolation and I cower.

Before,
I had seen shafts of light, both bright and filtered,
behind me,
around us.
But now . . . nothing.

Enveloped in the tight space of weighted midnight
my mind shifts to . . .
no, not panic,
simply an acceptance of despair,
where no stars wink, and nothing points the way

My breathing shallows;
Limbs, weak and loose, force me down.
On my own in this black, blank space
I sink,
my back to the door,
lock my arms around my knees,
rest my forehead on them
and fold into myself.

No surprise, really,
I admit I expected this -
to see nothing.

Part Three: The Art of Untying Knots

Fall 2001 – Winter 2006

Nothing changes until something moves
Einstein

"I attempted to rise, but was not able to stir: for as I happened
to lie on my back, I found my arms and legs were strongly
fastened on each side to the ground . . . I could only look
upwards . . . I heard a confused noise about me, but in the
posture I lay, could see nothing except the sky."
Jonathan Swift, Gulliver's Travels: Part I, Chapter I

Like Swift's awakening Gulliver
I discover I'm trapped.

Tied with a thousand tiny knots
that look too insignificant,
too familiar
to take seriously -

Silken and delicate at first,
roughened by question and struggle,
swollen by a wash of tears,
they hold fast.

Once I allowed . . . even welcomed most,
but then night fell
and I longed to see beyond,
to stretch,
to walk away.

Now, arms, legs and head pinned fast,
I can only stare upward -
following the outlines of memory tracing the sky.

Fall, 2001
Grace,

The disintegration of my marriage is a runaway train – lumbering, awkwardly veering from its familiar track while inevitably gathering speed. Couples counseling was all too brief – two sessions, two different therapists. I can only guess that BC is not hearing what he wants; he seems uninterested in pursuing much discussion while I am in the room. We are at cross purposes now: his grief is not the same as mine. As I continue struggling to come to terms with my own anguish, BC's emotional ride seems to have taken him much more quickly from sadness to impatience, from anger to neutrality. I sense he has no patience left for my needs, and rather than walk my journey with me, he is restless, anxious really, to make a new life on his own. Did I tell you he has already moved in with an old friend? I'm sorry if I repeat myself; I cannot seem to hold a coherent thought. He is coming to my office tomorrow; fear screams he will officially ask for the divorce.

I am operating in a maze of questions with no answers - a life so entirely full of uncertainty. Does BC realize the position in which his exit puts an already fragile me? Does he even care? Is there a way I can ever discover what he knows or thinks? Can I still trust the answers of one I entrusted my entire life to just a few short months ago? Really, Grace, I need this one answered now. Besides the disquiet it brings, is there actual danger in knowing and trusting nothing for sure?

Rilke in *Letters to a Young Poet* talks about moments of sadness as a tension that can astonish and paralyze us ". . . because everything we trust and are used to is . . . taken away from us; because we stand in the midst of a transition where we cannot remain standing." I am both astonished and paralyzed. The two most important males in my life have melted together into a yawning, aching space; they both have vanished. What am I to do besides continue the charade of one foot in front of the other?

Though Rilke goes on to indicate that one can't remain stationary within this tension of something vs nothing, I disagree. That's the space I inhabit; it's the space I own and remain. I've come to believe that the grieving never see themselves clearly, either in a mirror or through the eyes of others. Memories are always close. They rise to the surface unbidden and cloud any vision of the real, the present, the possible. Glimpse a direction ahead? Not from my vantage point.

There is one real thing I know with certainty: I have to leave this house. I absolutely cannot stay here alone and retain any semblance of sanity. This house is full of windows, yet any light is always gray. If the divorce is imminent as it seems to be, and someone has to live here while it's on the market, BC will need to move back once I'm gone. I hate leaving my darling cat – a loving, comfortable creature who has been with us our entire life together as a couple. His warm presence has been a lifesaver these last weeks, but I can't expect to move us both into - where? I must summon the energy to plan, to find a place to stay, to go somewhere safe and begin finding my footing.

I feel another Scarlett O'Hara moment coming on: I have to stop now and believe I can think and figure it all out tomorrow. I'll let you know where I am. Don't send any more mail to the house.

Jane

Fall, 2001

My dear son,

Your sister and a wonderful neighbor came over to help me pack today. After Christmas I have been invited to move in with a long-time and dear friend who will kindly provide me with my own bedroom, closet and bathroom – just enough to wrap me tightly in a cocoon. My choices will be narrowed, and with them my need to make decisions. I feel grateful; the less required of me, the better. Good decision-making is a past skill so I am keeping all possibilities to a minimum. Sharing space with someone gives me a reason to force my voice out loud, to eat, to remain alert to the living. I'm afraid to say all of this to anyone else – it sounds like whining to my own ears - so writing it to you helps me admit it quietly but resolutely to myself.

Anyway, back to the packing. As I remember, you didn't like moving, so the energy and anticipation of packing was never a pleasure for you as it has often been for me. But this time packing signals a free fall into the unfamiliar. No gravity, no tether, just a void. I'm kneeling before a long spacious closet that shelves family albums and boxes of treasures. One of those boxes holds my wedding dress and when I pull it out, the tears flow. So unaccustomed to being at a loss, without words, embarrassment creeps into my desolation. Your sister shuts the box and my neighbor holds out her arms to take it. She tells me with a gentle smile that she will keep it until I want to collect it. And *It* disappears with an easier smoothness than my memories.

Too quickly I am transported to my beautiful December wedding. I see your smile as you escort your grandmother down the aisle and later hear your wry laughter erupt during the reception; these recollections are as dear to me as the one I have of wearing that dress, dancing, laughing, planning for joys ahead. Because of my tears and the stops and starts of necessary decisions, it takes us hours to organize and box up what I'm to take away from this place that I called home for three years.

Others write and talk about being in contact with loved ones who have passed. Though I still serve my weak promises of your nearness, I haven't experienced a vision, dream or any spiritual expression as others write about. What do I need to do to bring you into my presence? Is it that I'm too unhappily rooted in this world to invite you properly? It appears I'm still a failure at bringing you home to me.

Mom

Winter, 2002

Dear Grace,

Your letter landed in my rented post office box, one more temporary thing that will have to serve my needs for awhile. I was with my Illinois family for the Christmas holiday and flew from there to be with a friend in Maryland; together she and I brought in my tenuous new year. As you probably remember, the kindness of friends has intervened and what I was hoping would transpire has; I won't have to go back to living alone for a while. I moved some clothing and necessities to a room provided by a long-time friend; BC condescended to move back into the house while it's on the market and to care for Lucas our cat.

I am now consistently scheduled with a therapist. A woman I think I would readily choose as a trusted friend, she patiently allows me to cry or simply sit silently when I can do nothing else. Her questions have brought me to life for a few hours this past month. Those same questions have led me to accept that I need an anti-depressant, so I am committed to working with her to find a pill or alternative therapy that might just carry some hope in it.

In answer to your gentle question, no, I can't say that hope is either a living presence or even a future thought. Doing life is a strain. I am too tied to the past I love, not free enough to vision or dream myself into another, more hope-filled space. To continue life, I know I have to move beyond this dark place but can still only give that need halfhearted attention.

I'm now forcing myself to journal. Though I'm told grief groups work well for some, I cannot imagine telling others what roils about in my heart now. I swear I'm breakable. Sitting in a circle with others to spew the ugliness I believe lives inside me is abhorrent. It terrifies me to think that after listening to others, then poking, prodding, and analyzing on my own, the success stories of others will only point me to the horror of my own inadequacy. What if a word or phrase of another leads me to believe that I could have done something differently to save my lost son or to revive either relationship? Or, worse yet, what if I discover I might have been able to extend Matt's life? I'm convinced I couldn't survive the guilt of realizing I turned left when I should have gone right – of discovering that more positive outcomes were possible and I didn't search or find them until it was too late.

If you can bring me anything through your prayers, let it be the grace of courage. Without that possibility, there is no next life chapter looming on my horizon. I only feel safe in isolation. My immediate plan is to get through the rest of this winter season, push myself to act like an aware and available mom and grandmother and walk through my working days with some competency. Those journal thoughts my therapist wants me to air and find voice for, should never be read. My latest entry: "what life is teaching me: it continues, nothing stands still and I hate it. I could not awaken tomorrow and it would be OK." I am wallowing shamefully in my own hopelessness.

This is one of those letters that should contain the *burn before reading* label. Make sure you throw this one away, my friend.

Jane

Winter 2002

Matt,

Sometimes I wonder why, but I'm still faithfully attending church and singing. Maybe it's because I don't see myself as so broken there. They hold up a mirror of how I looked before and I guess that helps me be ready for the next Monday morning. But I'm only there in flesh. I can't pray or even say the word, God. I no longer connect to the God who once fed my spiritual life. My latest questions for you: What is prayer, really? What can I expect if I do it?

I wish I had the power to change the way my mind fills with and then empties the same thoughts time after time. I wish I didn't find myself so tedious.

Mom

Almost Spring, 2002

Dear Grace,

I am practicing what to say when others ask me what happened between BC and me without crying or sounding anything besides delicately neutral. He has different needs now; he wants to move on; he feels we have grown apart; blah, blah, blah. I want to stay above the ugliness of it all in front of others, but there are times when my depression and pain lash out in unanticipated rage and I am taken aback. Driving, working alone, watching an inane commercial, listening to a beautiful ballad, reading – nothing is safe when this unbidden emotion surfaces. Most of the time I'm alone, so others aren't exposed to this raw side of me that continues to surprise. I've decided not to care whether it's a good thing or not – it just is.

BC and I continue to communicate about the house sale, counter offers, and selling our beautiful condo in the Rockies. Each email or call from him simply reminds me of what I am losing. And another hit came today: BC has given away our cat - the one *child* we, alone, loved and raised during all our years together - to someone I don't even know. This lovely animal was a beloved family member for so long, yet he could die without either of us close and loving. Guilt and anger combine in a volatile mix and here it is again – the rage borne of impotence.

I'm off to bed and am hoping for sleep; exhaustion and depression are restless bedfellows and my mind reels.
Jane

Spring, 2002
Grace,

First, let me thank you for being a steady presence in my life. Your notes and occasional calls during these last months keep me present to life beyond this self-imposed maze I faithfully and fretfully travel. I have spent these past months reliving the last sixteen years of my life with BC, working alone and with my therapist to disengage from both their embrace and their aching pain.

Endings and painful surprises have defined this month. Personally, my time shifts between being a ready and able mom, step-mom, and grandmother to those who are dear to me, and living as the recluse who voraciously reads, thinks and analyzes. Professionally, I walk through days trying not to trigger any damage to my students' learning or my own job security. On my best days I may appear adequate in both arenas but mostly I feel the weight of an imposter's clothes.

The ways my life have recently altered, as I repeat them neutrally, appear crushing even to me: I understand BC is already in another relationship, our divorce was finalized this week, my last home has sold. Reviewing this three-year relationship/divorce odyssey carries a biting, sharp freshness. A once seemingly endless journey, between the time BC first handed me the letter numbering his dissatisfactions and today's final period to our marriage, has really been life at mind-numbing speed.

This realization took me to my journal where I've just acknowledged some truths:

- I no longer know how to define what others might call a normal reaction to situations

- I have lost the desire to care about, but not the ability to be anxious about, most everything
- I no longer assume God has a place in my life
- Concentration and sleep are rare gifts
- My own death holds no fear

I need something lovely to surprise me - a sweet dream of my son, a hint at his contentment would be balm for an aching soul. Matt's birth date, both a dreaded and reverent event, is next week.

Jane

Spring, 2002

Dear Grace,

"For the Interim Time" in <u>To Bless the Space Between Us: A Book of Blessings,</u> is a lovely poem that moves its reader from raw realities to the blessings of possibilities. These few lines from author John O'Donohue's longer work remind me grief is not unique to me, a reminder I need at this lonely time. Yet, I find myself dwelling on its darker stanzas which so exactly mirror my present.

You are in this time of the interim
Where everything seems withheld.

The path you took to get here has washed out;
The way forward is still concealed from you. . . .

Everyone else has lost sight of your heart
And you can see nowhere to put your trust;
You know you have to make your own way through. . . .

Life is an untrustworthy commodity. Still achingly vulnerable, I'm unable to welcome, let alone ask for help. Who knows when the next loved one will leave, when those I let myself depend on will have had enough of my grieving? If I am to get through this, Grace, I am convinced it will mainly be on my own.

Gradually, you will learn acquaintance
With the invisible form of your departed;
And when the work of grief is done,
The wound of loss will heal . . .

Ah – this is where O'Donohue tries to push the presence of hope into my world, perhaps wanting to help me recall that all things really are possible when...or if trust returns.
Jane

Almost Summer, 2002
Dear Grace,

   My own personal roller coaster continues its ride with me bound tightly. Sometimes climbing, sometimes plummeting – it's as if the horrid thing has a mind of its own. And of course it does – that mind is mine. Without my own intervention I finally understand I'm destined to travel its ragged course until I work free from the memories and questions that keep me tied on.

As the months pass, I am letting myself experience some blessed higher, engaging times. Interesting university work, the energetic lives of my daughter, step children and grandchildren bring joy and laughter as well as challenge and a myriad of appealing reasons to concentrate on a life yet to unfold. In quieter, introspective times, forced by my own need to review, analyze and relive all that's happened, I note the coaster round a corner and nose down. With eyes screwed shut, I let hopelessness take me into another dive.

Themes of guilt, shame, loneliness, fear, and rejection hold sway in this place where the track can shift and dive so quickly. As a shadowy BC stands observing, I bring Matt's presence into my mind and hold imaginary, guilt-ridden conversations about my inability to bridge the monstrous gap between us before he died, my worry about his dying alone, my sadness about not being invited to his college graduation, my wondering if the relationship with his step-father somehow kept us apart - and the list goes on. After these dark monologues dissipate and they've both faded, I struggle to propel my thoughts forward, forcing the coaster to move toward another, slower upward loop.

Interestingly, some new thinking patterns are unfolding. Fueled by unpacking old perceptions and experiences with my therapist I'm gaining a bit of new-found righteous anger with small patches of clarity. I may be at a beginning of something important, an inkling of understanding that I am not solely at fault for BC leaving our marriage. I find such revelations send my coaster crawling upwards.

Luckily I am still living with my generous friend. She and I and her gentle, warmhearted dog have settled into routines that I find both safe and comfortable. Still, I realize a need to find my own place, to be on my own, and I'm shopping around. Moving on - tentatively and gingerly,

Jane

Summer, 2002

Hello Son,

I am in a mind/heart/soul place where I believe you have the spiritual presence to look in on me and know everything I do. Still I'm uncertain how to know or feel your presence as my reality and, as always, here I am squinting upwards for a sign to sense your approval, concern, or – whatever. It occurs to me that I could be trying too hard – like looking too closely for the spot on the butterfly's wing while never drawing back to witness the beauty of its wholeness. Don't know what to do about it, but it gives me pause to question the validity of all this endless self analysis. Are you rolling your eyes?

School is out for a few months so I have collected the time and courage to tackle an ever-growing stack of books in between house hunting. I just finished <u>When Bad Things Happen To Good People</u> by Rabbi Harold Kushner. He lost his son too. (Have you encountered his son - his son's spirit? Is that a ridiculous question? I am clueless about everything in your space.) Anyway, many of the Rabbi's words echo my thoughts about God and God's more modest place in my life. As early as page two he writes: "I believed that I was following God's ways and doing His work. How could this be happening to my family? If God existed, if He was minimally fair, let alone loving and forgiving, how could he do this to me?" Even if I persuade myself that I deserve the burden of your death, surely you, my brilliant, kind, and beautiful boy, never earned your painful path and early death. Why didn't God stop your suffering, intercede before your death?

The God I grew up with, provided to me by your grandparents, was all-powerful and wise and saw to it that everyone got what each deserved. I presumed that this God knew more about the world and justice than I ever could, so I was never led to wonder about the place death and loss had in my life, even when your grandfather died. But now, questions are all I have.

Last month, as soon as I finished reading Kushner's work, I sent the book to your grandmother, asking her to read and also comment as she read. As you remember, she is wise and so rooted and secure within her religious traditions that if anyone could help me unravel some of my questions about God, it is she. I underlined ideas that I wondered most about and highlighted passages for her response. We "talked" this way while she finished the book. In the end she sent me a typed overview of her thoughts and that helped a little; she also underlined different lines than I had, moving me into new directions of thought.

I am glad I asked for her help. I discovered she has been questioning her own understandings of life and death since you were taken; I would never have guessed that without these written conversations between us. Her take is that Kushner, like all of us who experience inexplicable loss, is simply trying to make sense out of the rules for living genuinely within a world of confusing complexities. Though not the *moral to the story* I was hoping for, the simplicity of that single idea serves to ground me. I find myself shifting back to O'Brien's thought about a true war story, which for me is the true grief story – " . . . if there's a moral at all, it's like the thread that makes cloth. . . . You can't extract the meaning without unraveling the deeper meaning. And in the end, really, there's nothing much to say . . . except maybe 'Oh.'"

Your grandmother sends her love.

Mom

Late Summer, 2002

Hey Grace, just a quick note –

I looked, I jumped, I landed!   Did you notice my new return address? I signed the papers just a few days ago to take ownership of a small but sweet patio home. Though I'm excited and feeling somewhat empowered by the courage I used to find and buy a place on my own, I remind myself that "on my own" is now the operative phrase.

Jane

Winter, 2002

My friend,

Holiday time again: A high school reunion, birthdays and Thanksgiving came and went; the semester finished and I will again train to Illinois to spend Christmas with Mom, my brother, sister-in-law and her extended family. This will be the fourth Christmas without Matt in my world, and my first as a new divorcee.

Day by day life stretches out in front of me, Grace. Friends are kind and work is all- consuming. The new house is in various stages of remodeling. My health is OK, most all of the physical issues having finally gotten as tired of doctor visits as their host. I trust the latest round of anti-depressants will see me through Christmas, helping me smile and respond on cue. But they are ugly – these feelings I haul around about my former husband and the decisions that have brought me to this place – my new normal, and I admit to a sharpened sense of abandonment and raw loneliness.

Jane

Winter, 2002

Matt,

Lukie died last week. I heard about it by accident from the woman BC gave him to for safekeeping a few months ago. She was taken aback by my surprise; she thought BC would have let me know. He didn't. I remember with nostalgic tears the times Luke allowed you to wrestle with him on the floor without either claws or teeth to fend you off. He was a gentle, patient, beautiful giant of a cat who deserved to be loved into the next life. If it is possible, please welcome him with great celebration, son, and whisper to him that I am sorry he was abandoned by those who loved him. Like you, he died alone, without me close. I hope he's found his way to you. I love you both.

Mom

Winter, 2002

Outside my window is dark, son, and though I want to give you a smile, tell you I'm looking ahead to new beginnings, a new year, I can't. What am I being taught with all this introspection, all the striving to regain my balance? Doing life is like walking around with a thorn in my heel – its ache vexes and blunts the kindnesses of anything I might find joyful; its throbbing seeps into daily existence, demanding my attention. At one time I would have tried to pray it away but those times are gone. Like poet Sylvia Plath, "I talk to God but the sky is empty." Prayer and its God are no longer my tools for thorn extractions. What now son?

Winter, 2003
Happy New Year Grace

Zora Neale Hurston, wise Southern author writes, "There are years that ask questions and years that answer." Today is a day that finds me hoping that 2003 is a year for questions with softer edges and answers loaded with possibilities. I like that I have enough hope this January day to believe I might again have a say in the shaping of my own life. Though there's no doubt I'm still bound, when I only focus on today rather than the past or future, I rest fairly comfortably on the coaster - its trajectory a placid inching forward.

It is always healing to spend time with my family and away from the places where I come face to face with a former life. I had a long round-trip train ride to Illinois, rested well, and then enjoyed the company of those who quietly and unconditionally love me. No questions to answer and no plans to describe – just time to be quiet with no explanations. Mom is physically stronger now and appears happier, more acclimated to her assisted-living housing. I have a greater sense of calm when I know she is stable and closer to caregivers. Now home, I resolve to discover ways of welcoming and practicing the peace that I let myself embrace during the visit.

Right now – because I can't think beyond this moment – I'm struck with this urgency to establish a new way of being. My newest plan is to hang out in some book stores, to wander the shelves and continue to find how others have learned to live within the grip of sadness and loss. Though I started doing that earlier, I ran out of the energy to continue. Time to try again. I resonate with the ideas of the Czech poet Rainer Maria Rilke. His words rarely fail to uplift me and provide food for new thought. Love the following because it keeps me in my most hopeful place: "And now let us welcome the New Year – Full of things that have never been."

So, dear friend Grace, not to worry as I turn more of my attention inward. I am about analyzing the vagaries of my particular grief journey in hopes of untying some of its complexities. Does that mean I want to get a little control of my life again – of course! You may do a mental eye roll if you'd like, but I long for a modicum of predictability, of balance around those "things that have never been." For some reason I think peace might trail behind. I'll try to temper my need with a powerful and healthier new reality: one is never really in control. I've grown painfully aware that roller coaster living does not endear itself to control-minded riders. Now concentrating on resources to help me craft a plan to hop off the damn thing.

Jane

You can't prevent birds of sorrow flying over your head –
But you can prevent them from building nests in your hair
Chinese Proverb

Winter, 2003

Hello my son,

With new readings and conjecturing crowding my thinking, I am full of questions for you. Were you a Buddhist rather than a Christian when you died? Did you embrace both ideas? Were you simply a student of all religions rather than a believer in any? What ideas did your study help you embrace about ethics, mortality, God? The way you chose to live and the isolation in your dying continue to plague me; I'm looking for ways to learn and cope. Having some grasp of your head and heart-felt belief systems can only help. If you did believe or find serenity in some sort of faith or tradition, it would empower me to picture your passing with more peace. No matter what the belief or non-belief, if your time alone those last hours was filled with a philosophy, a theory of your own mortality, I could rest knowing fear was not the last emotion to fill you. You had lived in your brilliant mind for so many years, pondering the unfolding of such a heady idea as mortality would have kept you company. Understanding the Matthew of those last hours might help me actually let your ideas take my place as your comforter.

When your dad and sister and I cleared out your modest room during that September day, I took some of your books with me. I was not surprised, son, to note that you had as many books as any other type of possession. The Bible I gave you, a few well-worn novels, a tape discussing the philosophical wisdom of Joseph Campbell, a text on world religions - all pieces of your life I now mix with mine. Why were those the ideas you kept? How did their messages impact you?

When you began in earnest to study philosophy, you talked about religious and philosophical traditions and their impact on the human condition. Buddhism came up in our conversations, so I began to wonder more about its allure for you. Just lately I've screwed up the courage to begin digging deeper into the pile of your last belongings. I admit I have to force myself to look through your things; touching and rearranging them brings the twist of melancholy. Still, using your cache of books and some I'm collecting about loss, death and dying, I'm committed to continue my search for awareness. I know I could get farther, faster, with your intercession. How about a wake-up call? A visitation? I could use whatever you've got for me.

Mom

PS: I read something in Breathnach's <u>Simple Abundance Daybook</u> today and am led to believe that delving into your philosophical ideas now is the right thing to do. She notes that we humans continue to wait until the elusive *tomorrow* to live fully, but that life is always unforeseen circumstances, always change. Instead of waiting for the *right time* to do things, she reminds me to create that right time now.

Coincidence is God's way of remaining anonymous.
Einstein

Winter, 2003
Dear Matt,

It is between semesters and I've had time to do some reading and thinking. Much of the reading brings me more questions for you, while others resonate to the point of a "yes, I can see that" nod. Since you were immersed in Eastern philosophies/religions, my newest exploration makes me feel a stronger connection to you. A subtle shift is taking place and instead of wallowing in the fear and dread that used to mar my convictions about those hours you lay alone, dying, my mind is beginning to overlay a new vision, one that holds less pain and guilt.

Let me try this newest consideration out on you: if you found meditation as well as the detachment and heightened perceptions these philosophies have been touted as providing, you might have already clearly understood your own impermanence, your own inevitable death, long before it happened. I can't quite visualize you in meditation. Did you struggle with or quietly discover the belief that human life can only have full meaning when it is lived in full acceptance of death? I am guessing that in time you accepted this with a knowing smile. Might it actually be possible that you met Death that September day as an expected friend rather than a dreaded opponent? I long for that as truth. Death, who took you from me, has been a hated opponent for over four years; I'm unable to lay that burden down.

I'll bet you are familiar with the "Parable of the Mustard Seed." The mother in this story grieves uncontrollably over the death of her beloved son and carries his corpse everywhere in search of a remedy to Death's visit. Unable to accept that death is terminal, this mother searches for an antidote to administer to the son in her arms. She meets the Buddha and begs for help. Instead of providing a healing, he instructs she go from house to house in search of a few grains of mustard seed, part of the necessary antidote. The catch is that she may not accept a mustard seed from any household in which no one has ever died. In time, of course, this mother comes to know that death is inescapable and finally, peacefully, surrenders her son to the fires of cremation.

Reading and thinking about what you had been contemplating the last few years of your life gave me a new perspective. According to my understanding, the Buddha counsels that humans should not make any plans in this world without reckoning with death; everything will be parted from what it desires in the end. If you accepted that and found some kind of profound awareness of your own death, believing that a type of freedom awaited you, I need to uncover a way to no longer carry you in my arms from house to house, situation to situation, searching for ways to bring you back. I'm not able to surrender you.

To do more than only survive, but move with some hope into my own healing I'm compelled to continue drinking in, deliberately and consciously, new ways to achieve grace, peace and balance. Your beliefs tell me to stop fighting with Death. To do that I have to know that as you were dying you neither longed for nor feared death, but simply accepted its presence with a calm, open mind and heart. That vision of a grace-filled parting is certainly more welcome than the other I have been carrying.

I love you

Mom

Be patient with all that is unsolved in your heart and try to love the questions themselves. Do not now seek the answers which cannot be given you because you would not be able to live them and the point is to live everything. Live the questions now . . . you will gradually . . . live your way into the answers.
Rainer Maria Rilke

Spring, 2003

Dear Grace,

The first university semester is over and the second is in full swing. These past months, busily living in present moments, I have been doing pretty well on the coaster – riding a center loop with minimal turns and shifts, and easier swings around all the corners. Because I've taught my classes a few times now the curriculum is more familiar, I've had the time to devote more awareness to the people in my personal life. And with that additional time comes an altering in the ride.

Reading and studying about loss now combine with watching it happen again. The young family of one of my stepson's is coming apart. I'm trying to be available to both the adults and my grandchildren but it is incredibly difficult to walk into this situation with any objectivity. It tosses me back into something all too familiar and sad – and ugly. I'm clear that my own slim resources are unequal to the task of doing much to help. I have very little to give to any of them besides a listening ear or cup of tea. The situation feels too close and throws me off balance. Of course I have taken on the guilt of, once again, not being enough, which may sound silly to you but nonetheless is true.

The coaster turns downward.

But there are some readings that are activating hope. Cognitively I have always known that others share the pain of grief journeys, and though the wisdom of this knowledge has knocked on my heart's door before, it is just now that I notice that door is ajar. The more I read of grief, the death of other children and loss of beloved partners, the more I become aware of the blinders of focused, personal pain I've worn. Since BC left our marriage I have mostly fixed my gaze onto tracing memory. Peripheral vision takes more energy than I've had but am starting to note an ability to refocus my attention - beyond the memories, the pain of what is lost - and when I'm present to it I feel heartened by such delicate, subtle changes. The coaster stutters and slows.

But wait – there's more. The school district is terminating its present teaching partnership agreement with the university - and my job with it. I move to a district high school with new curriculum expectations, to teach a different level of student next year. I'm back in the public school world starting in August. My meeting with the school district administrator who told me of the upcoming shift brought with it all too familiar feelings of imbalance and loss. I could feel my fragile equilibrium tip into a downward slide and the most tenuous me watches as rejection and fear join hands, leap aboard and join me on the roller coaster. If I had a free hand I'd pop a Dramamine - feeling pretty queasy with the up and down of it all right now.

Thanks for the invitation to visit this summer, but I need to decline. I expect to use most of the summer months reading literature and planning lessons for the new job. If I do anything beyond prepping for work it will be either riding the rails to Illinois to spend time with Mother, being a more available mom and grandma, or maybe even taking a long weekend in the mountains to continue some solitary reading and thinking.

Have a good summer. I'll be in touch.

Jane

Summer, 2003

Grace,

As you guess by the date, school is finally out and I've said my good-byes to university colleagues. I have a pile of new textbooks and author ideas to ingest before I can start all those new lesson plans. And, I have children to nurture, chaos to calm and issues to unpack for understanding, maybe even some advice to pose. I guess I won't wean myself off the anti-depressant just yet.

I retreated to Lamott's <u>Traveling Mercies</u> during a coffee break this morning and found this rather interesting idea: the Buddhists believe when a lot of things become unbalanced or start unraveling all at once, it is to protect something big and lovely that is trying to get itself born. That something needs for us to be distracted so it can be born as perfectly as possible – without our imperfect help. I am attracted to this interesting idea. And isn't it a great thing that in the midst of both accepted risks and unanticipated change I can still be enticed by hope? Anyway, if this idea has any truth in my life, something pretty darn amazing is taking shape as I write. I wonder if I will recognize it when/if it appears. Keeping my eyes and ears open . . .

Jane

Fall, 2003
Grace,

Summer is gone! What is it with time! When you want more, you always have less – when you want it to race forward, it drags!

I just learned that BC moved to Arizona to begin a new position. Evidently he is relocating. I am relieved that I need no longer worry about running into him in town – hate to admit it, but the thought of that terrifies me. Don't have a clue what I would say to one who was once my entire life and now probably considers me simply a personal, historical footnote of sorts. Small talk? Just not ready to sort all that our right now but only acknowledge it as a coaster turn.

I am in meetings with new public school teaching teammates preparing for students who arrive this week. Life will become incredibly busy in the next few days and, if my past public school teaching experience is any indication, time to myself is a luxury of the past. As soon as I settle my professional life into its routine, I'll let some personal needs crawl forward. I'm thinking after the first months of second semester, life might slow down a little. Until then, I am my work.

I'm determined to carve out personal reading time as soon as possible. Cognitively, I realize I need to be more than a parent who has lost a child or a woman who was left by a husband. Clearly I don't know yet how to emotionally become more than those two things, but I believe life will hold little genuine joy until I do. Ongoing therapy and anti-depressants are tools I am choosing to use to re-build, and though I've discovered admitting to either of these sometimes makes me feel like a powerless, ineffectual weakling, I am resigned to accept both in my life as fact, as necessary.

I'm continuing to collect and stack on the bedside table the ideas and teachings of others; those, added to the inevitable papers I'll be grading, loom as my immediate future. Don't expect much from me for quite a while, Grace. I'm gearing up for the wild ride of being a new learner in the midst of high school teaching.
Jane

Winter, 2003
Dear Matt,

I took some holiday time to rearrange all the resources on death and dying I've been gathering. My book pile is growing but any energy for study is being spent at school. First semester is over and I'm catching the train in a few days to spend Christmas with your grandmother, aunt and uncle. I miss spending holiday time with your sister, but staying here is so hard. I worry that I am setting a tradition of not celebrating an important time with her; I don't want that to happen but am still lost in the need to be away from this place where you were last with me. One more issue to unpack and face as life.

As I shifted books around, those I kept from your room surfaced and I re-discovered the worn and marked copy of Immanuel Kant's Critique of Pure Reason. Leafing through it brings me to your handwritten notes, the pages you had dog-eared, the starred words, phrases and sentences you thought important. It's the first time I've seen your handwriting in so long. In my mind I sketch your face and smile, your lovely long fingers holding the pencil; I bury my face in the fold of the book and breathe in all of you that's left to me.

Did pure reason help you prepare for your own death? I wish I understood where, who, you are now. All this work - the reading, the thinking, the reaching for understanding about why you had to die when you did – I have to believe is for a reason but that reason still eludes me. What would your Kant offer about the connections between death and pure reason? I don't have the energy to unpack them right now, but it would be so like you to have a ready answer.

Come visit me and we'll talk. More aptly, you'll explain and I'll listen.
Mom

Winter, 2004
". . . between one dip of the pen and the next, the time passes: And I hurry, I drive myself, and I speed toward death. We are always dying – I while I write, you while you read, and others while they listen or block their ears; they are all dying."

Petrarch's words resonate deeply within me, Grace. We are all journeying toward the same end. The quality of the travel time is where I'm compelled to direct more energy. I am resolved to live this new year finding ways to cut the many knots that still bind me to the aching sadness of the past.

Is this life theme as tedious for you as it is for me? Then move ahead!! I hear that message yelled into my most rational head space and literally jerk at the metaphoric knots around my wrists and ankles. My head tells me I'm ready but fearful thoughts, overwhelming mistrust of myself and others, and recalling yet another vulnerable, personally joyless year so easily crowd out the more positive judgments I'm learning to nurture. Introspection, ad nausea – Enough!

F. Scott Fitzgerald wisely mused, "You don't write because you want to say something; you write because you've something to say." I've nothing new to say, Grace, so I'm going off radar until I do.

Jane

Winter, 2004

My dear, wise philosopher,

I discovered Thich Nhat Nanh's <u>Living Buddha, Living Christ</u>. Quiet times now find me reflecting on my lapsed affection for God and haltingly making connections between that older reality and new observations about Buddhism. Am I supposed to build something in between?

The God who I understood was in all things – the blanket of shining stars, the allowance of both fair and unethical business deals, the tides moving away from beached whales and into drowning homes, the elation and anxiety of love affairs, the gratitude in a full head of hair, the random kindnesses of one stranger to another, the wonder of childbirth – is the same God who was on duty at your death, the master of ceremonies at your two memorial services. Fascinating – the same God equally companions all the good and all the ugly. What am I to make of that?

Though I'm clear I will never again be able to relate to a deity who requires the memorization and recitation of chapter names in a holy book, or demands a subservience to the human-made codes of right religious conduct, or expects me to believe that your untimely death was simply fate, what am I to trust? Once it was comforting: if God was in control, I didn't have to be; prayer from good people produces heavenly results; enter God and enter hope – but no more.

Mom

Spring, 2004

Son,

My therapist, who I think you might like because she asks great questions and speaks kindly of you, suggests I take some time to define goals for our sessions. What do I want to accomplish? Really? Accomplish more? I'm getting up to go to work, eating, not isolating so much, focusing ahead (well, sometimes). Enough – right? I have no answer for either of us.

Your grandmother turns ninety today and you, thirty-four, tomorrow. Both these milestones give me pause to reflect on how time, really an artificial construct, continues to rule my thoughts, feelings and behaviors. This time of the year you are on my mind, even more than usual. Your birth date is both celebrated and grieved – a tough dichotomy to juggle. Your grandmother's arrival at such a grand number is to be celebrated, even though because of that number, her physical and mental states continue to deteriorate. The longer we humans live, an aspect we desire, the more needy we become, a quality many of us hate. And therein lies the rub. I lost you too early and will lose my mother long after she discovers, and lives within, her own frustrating and often painful, limitations.

All in all, for me, time means loss. I have aging and time issues, and I hate it. The older I get, the farther I travel from when we were together. The older I get, the less time I have to heal, to learn to trust again, to create healthy boundaries; the older I get, the more difficult it is to believe that relationship and intimacy are possible for me. I'm writing this to you because it embarrasses me to say it aloud. Your mom is a woman who always believed she would be able to grow older and wiser more gracefully, but she is doing neither because Time, like Death, is a detestable enemy.

Yeah, I know - sounds like I just may have a goal or two to work toward after all.

Mom

Summer, 2004

Dear Grace,

Just a note because I really have little to give you, but since there are some positives, you deserve to hear a smiling voice for a change.

I have finally officially retired from the school district and will move permanently to the university setting at the end of the summer. I'm looking forward to returning to the higher education realm as those curricular and instructional challenges seem to suit me more happily. At the same time, I'm working on a chapter for a text being compiled and edited by a university colleague. I felt complimented to be asked. It will be my first published manuscript. Generally I feel as if I am able to be a more present mom and grandma now. When I laugh with those I love it is coming from my more genuine and open heart.

I'm dating! Another first! We've been seeing each other for a few months and I enjoy his company. Trusting myself to participate in any (let alone, healthy) relationship is an issue, so I'm taking everything really slowly. The family is throwing a 90th birthday party for Mother in a few weeks so I'm flying back to help to create the celebration. I've invited him to come – big step! And, drum roll: I am finally off the anti-depressant.

I'm living in my own skin without the aid of a pill. The timing feels right.

So far 2004 is holding balance for me - and even though I'm still tied in place, the roller coaster heads benignly forward, the knots easing slightly. Optimism, a very old but mostly-absent friend, whispers a lighter, brighter horizon beckons.

Jane

Winter, 2004

Dearest boy,

"Practice makes perfect." "Practice makes permanent." "If you believe something long enough, it will come true." "Pretend long enough and it will be fact." 2004 has been a year of much practice and some pretense. I tell the woman who faces me in the mirror that good things fill her days and optimism is really not one of life's ironies. Then I look for her smile, either forced or genuine, and with it fixed in place, feel strong enough to be on my way. Lots of conscious effort goes into practicing, through what I say and how I appear, the beliefs that I am getting better, that grief will not define me for the rest of my life, and that chaos is fertile enough to grow something beautiful and hopeful. I admit to being a little proud of myself – I persevere in the midst of the complexity that is my grief.

I found this short fable and trusted you would understand why it spoke to me:

A man who took great pride in his lawn
found himself with a large crop of dandelions.
He tried every method he knew
to get rid of them. Still they plagued him.

Finally he wrote the Department of Agriculture.
He enumerated all the things he had tried
and closed his letter with the question:
"What shall I do now?"

In due course the reply came: "We suggest you
learn to love them "

A. deMello, The Song of the Bird

It has been six years since you left my world, three years since I let myself open to the grief of your loss, and still you haven't spoken to me. It may be that I don't recognize you when you try to visit, or I'm still too self-absorbed to notice you beyond my own willful, intermittent tears. But I am better now, son, with ears that are opening and a heart that is unfolding. The dandelions are welcome to bloom.

Mom

Winter, 2005

Hi Grace,

Funny thing, hope: I know I'm in its presence when I feel courageous. I'm beginning to write poetry again. Matt's life and death are my subjects; healing and catharsis, my purposes. I'm flying solo with no extra anti-d chemicals on board. Children and grandchildren seem relatively balanced, work is moving along as expected and I am finally in a space where I feel confident enough to extend a little trust to life. Yes, for me, bravery is indeed hope in action.

Still remembering Fitzgerald's statement and hoping to produce "something to say."

Jane

Spring, 2005

My dear and patient friend,

The roller coaster has been turning and during the quieter times of the ride, I've been busy trying to loosen those tethers. Throughout last summer and now as the months move into the lighter days and times of early spring, I have welcomed personal reading back into my days. Always voracious, my appetite for losing myself in a book has grown even larger. At first I could only read escapist novels; crawling into a mystery and letting the bad, the bold and the wise find their way in and out of puzzles is still wonderfully distracting. Happily, I've progressed to the point of being able to navigate back and forth from those to nonfiction starring the brave – those who have journeyed well through loss, somehow learning how to create an open and genuinely honest lifestyle after suffering.

About half of the time my mind and heart are open enough to listen to and learn from the author. In an ever-growing stack of books are Kubler-Ross's <u>On Death and Dying</u> and <u>Death: The Final Stage of Growth</u> as well as Kushner's <u>When Bad Things Happen To Good People</u>. There are nuggets of what I am growing into calling my *truth* in each of them. I was drawn to a chapter in one of Kubler-Ross's book by the inescapable veracity of its title: "Dying Is Easy, But Living Is Hard." She writes in its introduction what is one of my truths: "Learning to reinvest yourself in living when you have lost someone you love is very difficult but only through doing so can you give some meaning to that person's death."

Another book that caught my notice and called me to reading it was Catherine Sanders's <u>How to Survive the Loss of a Child</u>. She unpacks her five-phase grief cycle a bit differently than Kubler-Ross. This cycle provided me a more comprehensible and personal way to view my own processing of the loss of Matthew and my marriage. Sanders affirms we are never the same people we were before a loss; we are most basicaslly who we are right at this moment – another absolute truth for me.

Let me give you the short course: Phase 1 is *Shock*; Phase II, *Awareness of Loss*; Phase III is called *Conservation/Withdrawal*; Phase IV, *Healing*; and Phase V, *Renewal*. As I read about the cycles I see myself squarely within *Conservation/Withdrawal;* even though I know I'm growing stronger, I can easily find myself slipping into that all-too-familiar draining sense of fatigue, futility and despair. Self-imposed isolation is still only a word or touch or page away. What feels most restorative, however, is trusting that *Healing,* closing the wounds and opening to new identities, is waiting for me - if one can reasonably count on such phases of chaos actually having an order.

It is a hopeful place – looking with some confidence at the possibility that forgiveness is more than an abstraction. If you think any of these titles or ideas will be helpful to other friends who are riding grief's roller coaster, please pass them on.

Courage is not such a strange concept now, but clarity? Now that still requires intercession.

Jane

Spring, 2005

Dear Matt,

You loved word play. Your clever mind molded and engineered words into amusements. After biking, I might call it your best sport – spinning ideas using the power of your words. Perhaps now, since I'm a little stronger, I should pull out one of your notebooks and read what was happening in your mind, your life, when you were away from me. Maybe . . .

I still obsess about what I think was a reticence to share with me. Discovering you shared more of yourself with people you knew for months than you did with me, hurts. See, this is one of the toeholds that make the climb out of the pit so difficult: I still don't know what I did to push you away. For the sake of sanity I have to believe something happened to us – I said something wrong or I didn't show up some place when I should have or - whatever – and we each took that experience off to our own corners of perception. Then we created our separate, individual, personal relationship myth. Once you physically went away, once the disease seemed to direct your choices, once you decided that I needed somehow to be spared your pain, you left me. That is my myth, my perception of our final mother/son years. Am I close to yours?

How much responsibility should I carry of this, son? Help me out with this one because I am having a very hard time sorting it all out and moving beyond it. I have to get this one figured out. Is there a shelf life for this guilt? Another five years? Ten? My lifetime? Will I recognize the right timing to untie these bonds that hold me to guilt, to more easily lift up my head and heart, to finally believe my unconditional love for you was realized and accepted across all those miles between us?

Please visit my dreams. Like then, your Mom is here now – waiting.

Fall, 2005

Hello Son,

I found the following quote in <u>Death Be Not Proud</u>. The author's wife, Frances Gunther, shares how she makes some sense of living on this earth after the death of her son: "Look Death in the face. To look death in the face and not be afraid. To be friendly to Death as to life. Death as a part of life, like Birth. Not the final part. . . .

Look Death in the face; it's a friendly face, a kindly face, sad, reluctant, knowing it is not welcome but having to play its part when its line is called, perhaps trying to say 'Come, . . .I understand how you feel, but come – there may be other miracles!' . . ."

I count looking death in the face as a very enlightened response from a grieving mother. I might play, fleetingly, with such an idea, but know that I would need to back away when our faces – Death's and mine - get too close. To contemplate that Death is not the final, saddened word, but might actually show up with a friendly face when it introduces itself to us mortals is totally unfamiliar territory.

Always searching for a way to stretch my boundaries and tease out answers to ever-present questions, I've decided to look into finding ways to introduce the most comfortable tendrils of my Christian roots to this newer, more fearless way of thinking about conducting myself in both life and death. I want a look at those *other miracles* Gunther mentions. I want to provide a place where my spirit can expand into soaring – or at least smiling. This quest brought me to writer and teacher Wayne Dyer, and his work called <u>Manifest Your Destiny</u>. With so many hours behind me of analyzing the paths I traveled and experiences I endured, imagine my surprise at being asked by the author to rest my brain.

According to Dyer, we all need to look beyond the mind to not only heal, but to also more fully walk our day-to-day existence. The *Spiritual* does not grow within the *Intellectual*. The author prods us to notice and then open to miracles by tuning into the love and inspiration available in our own hearts. Oh my – I haven't felt like trusting my heart for many years. It seems I have to let go of one of the only things I've trusted – my intellect – to discover . . . well, I'm not sure. Some sort of trust, of peace, would be nice.

I wait for you Matt. Fresh waves of hopelessness still break to drag me back and daily living only emphasizes the fact that you aren't with me. It's hard to surrender to new ideas.

Your mom

Fall, 2005

Grace,

Just a note to follow up your card: my delicate patchwork of personal balance is unraveling. How is it possible that the sharp twists and turns of this journey can still surprise even a veteran traveler? When will I learn that the only constant I can count on is the unknown, the unexpected?

Even though I thought my physical issues had settled into a healthy balance, evidently I was wrong. I don't feel well - neither eating nor sleeping much; the doc needs some more blood to untangle what's going on with me. And, yes, Mom's poor health resurfaced. After a pretty good spell, she started shifting downhill not too long after our 90th birthday celebration this past summer. I wish we could find the brakes for her fast-failing ability to continue walking without pain or worry of falling.

Yes to still dating, but things aren't turning out as I hoped so right now it is periodic at best. Frankly I don't have the trust or patience to let anything special unfold. At this point I expect pursuing relationship will take the emergence of a brave, intuitive man, one who would happily just read my mind. It is too much work to unpack the complex me to another. Work is fine; a university colleague and I are flying to Montana to facilitate a workshop for a small school district. Nice to be asked but hard to engage in the real-life preparation.

My poetry project is more in charge of me than the other way around. Sometimes images and their meanings simply pour out and I scramble for paper; others times I just sit and stare through a sheet of blankness, waiting for a muse. No matter what I produce, I'm in tears. I form a visual of Matt to write of him and though the results of this poetic experience are authentic and often gratifying, actually creating the lines and verses through these pictures are incredibly painful. I'm pretending it's important to do, a tool for healing and personal growth, with the hope that such pretense will become reality. This writing is the hardest thing I've ever forced myself to do, and in dark times wonder if this exercise is more masochistic than productively cathartic. I'm again caught in my obsession to produce something from and with this emotional, psychic and, too often, physical pain. Once

again, I've disappointed myself and Fitzgerald by
spending time on nothing worth saying.

Jane

Winter, 2006

Your latest phone message alerted me that someone
shared my hospital visit with you. Shortness of breath,
weak knees, ambulance ride, heart monitor, hours at the
hospital – all a bit of *sound and fury* indicating nothing of
substance yet. I'll be sporting a portable heart monitor
for a couple of weeks to get some baseline data and if
there is anything beyond normal to tell you, I'll give you
a call. I've acquiesced to this last test only to bring others
peace. I have no doubt I'm physically fine. All doctors
involved are suggesting I go back to the anti-depressant.

Mostly, Grace, this incident leaves me in the all-too
familiar space of wanting directions for untying knots and
finding answers to questions not only about my physical
health, but now also about the mind/body - combining the
brain and the heart. Cognitively, I have long been aware
of this interconnectedness within ourselves, but it has
only been at the analytical level; now I'm moving it to a
very personal level. The timing of this episode is too
close to the latest roller coaster plummet and loss of
balance to be coincidence. As soon as I feel a little better
I'm going to begin searching beyond any physical tests to
discover why my heart aches.

The holiday was as always: a loving and worried
family drawing together to hold up those in need. I

always miss time with my daughter and grandchildren, but as long as Mother is alive, this trip is what I must do. Loneliness, vulnerability, and even shame that I'm still muddling along alone, settle their considerable bulk next to me in the coaster.

The very air around me feels heavy. I'm in an Elizabethan play and squinting ahead, I spy a formidable soothsayer heading right at me. More later -
Jane

Winter, 2006
Son,

Night falls early in February and Fridays bring with them a stretch of unstructured hours to fill. It was into a darkening February Friday that your stepfather resurfaced. I opened my mailbox to find a package addressed in your stepfather's hand. My heart stuttered, the coaster lurched and I closed my eyes and heart to what I thought could only be inevitable pain.

It wasn't until the next day that I was strong enough to actually open the mailer. Packed with pictures and papers, it rained unwelcome memories. Not unwelcome because they are ugly or obscure or even complex, but unwelcome because of the stinging of unfulfilled yearning they bring. Family pictures spill over my lap – your laughing face during a Christmas Eve at our old home; your stepfather's silliness captured during a family dinner; a collection of travel photos marking happy summers, the tracing of grandchildren born, growing from diapers into primary school plays and soccer tournaments, and more - and more. Each photo transports me to its time and place. They reframe the times and people I no longer have, those who grow older without my touch, those who I can no longer hold as mine.

The family albums I retained from the divorce have stayed packed away. Even though new measures of strength and hope surface periodically in everyday life, I just didn't think I was ready to unpack and set free all the memories. I can't trust my heart; reliving happy times still has the power to define sadness so those precious albums remain sealed and out of sight. This surprise package forces me into the core of my worst fear – a viewing of the former happiness of a now-broken family and grieving your death anew.

If it were only Monday, life would have a structure, familiar boundaries, and my feelings, moved to that already-overflowing place called "on hold," could remain at bay. But it's Saturday. Hours unfold before me with no plan other than reliving, sensing and anticipating the many textures of loss.

Mom

Winter, 2006

Grace,

As I expected, physically my heart is fine. I said yes to another round of anti-depressants and am beginning to delve into the world of spirit and meditation. Though I continue to sing and faithfully attend church, neither fills my soul as often or as fully as they once did. I've decided to add this spiritual practice as a different way to worship - a way to meet, in Dyer's (Manifest Your Destiny) words, "a point where peace serves as a serene substitute for doubt and anxiety."

As I understand it, Buddhists believe that the ways to peace and joy begin when one looks deeply into their own suffering because hiding painful realities can never give one the full picture of life. Learning and accepting all realities is purported to bring a kind of relaxation and relief as we no longer have to pretend. I'll start my fledgling meditation efforts with looking deeply into my own sadness. Does not sound like a way to ease into a peace-filled, spiritual practice to me, but what do I know.

I'm still writing, still reading, still teaching, and still putting one foot in front of the other.

Jane

April, 2006

Hello my son - I saw you! I felt your presence! You were standing straight and at ease - and your smile - oh, that impish grin! It was wonderful to wake from my dream into the midst of such calm. Though I can't recall actual words, the impression of your spirit is indelible. We're close again. You know you are loved. I promise not to analyze why I was finally open to this dreaming experience, but only to bask in the light of you within me, of this shared intimacy. I think you may have just changed my life's direction again.

Mom

April, 2006

It is your birthday month, son, and having you return to me this month reminds me of the mixed sweet and painful intimacies of birth. Do you remember that time? If you do, let me just begin with an apology. This letter is a confession of sort and is, in its unfolding, as much for me as for you. Together we brought you into this world but I want you to know that I am more present with you now than I was during that hazy and somewhat chaotic time we spent birthing you.

It was the 70's; as always I had done my homework and was determined to have an enlightened birthing experience. Great breathing techniques were practiced and I thought I was devouring the most aware reading about giving birth as naturally as possible. But I was so self-absorbed about it all. I hadn't come to think of you as more than just, you know, a baby! How much could you participate? It was so all about me; you were in second place.

In human calendar terms, you were late. What I finally understand is that you weren't late, but right on your time. I just didn't get it then. Time, that human construct keeping us all in its arbitrary rhythm, often forces rather than allows. I wish I had appreciated that fact when you were so clearly luxuriating inside me.

Anyway, you were my first and I was scared and, so like me then, impatient. Your grandmother was waiting to join us as soon as you were born and I wanted help from someone who apparently knew a lot more than I or your dad did. And, I'll admit it; I was mighty uncomfortable lugging you around. So, I decided to take some steps to get you out of me so we could start the next stage in my life; see how self-absorbed I really was? How did you survive me with such humor and grace anyway?

I read that physical activity stimulates labor. I was awkward (never my favorite way to be as you know) but could still do housework. I decided to get on my hands and knees and wash the kitchen floor. As expected, this up and down, back and forth pushing motion annoyed you enough to get labor started and land me in a hospital bed. You were twelve hours in arriving and more than once I rethought the whole deal. Had I the choice at that time, you, my dear, could have had permanent residence inside, if you promised to not grow one more ounce.

I felt rotten at your birth – so tired; the princess in me totally violated. You, of course, were perfect. Beatific, calm, a soul destined to change my life and teach me wonderful secrets about living through both your short, joy-filled and challenging life, and your unexpected death. Here are some things our beginning and our present have taught me:

- Late and early are merely human constructs, only important if one makes them so

- Be Present - interact with no expectation to control
- No pushing!
- Life has its own rhythm; one can either fight or flow

Please be happy with me that I've learned enough about what is important in my life to realize I actually needed to apologize. Now I promise you I will figure out how to live fully, to trust my intuition, and to relish life one day at a time. I gave you life in human form. You open me to ideas about life beyond those boundaries and my love overflows.

Mom

> "Not knowing when the dawn will come,
> I open every door."
> *Emily Dickinson*

Summer, 2006

Dear friend,

School is out and time abounds: I feel a freedom that almost unties me from my personal coaster ride. I'm taking the time to celebrate the fun, busy and productive lives of my daughter and grandchildren, to catch playtime with friends, to work out, read, write and even practice meditating. I have set up a meeting with an acquaintance, who is also a publisher, about the poetry project. I think Matt wants me to write and publish something about my grief journey and so I have decided to get brave and talk with someone about the possibility. I hate thinking about anyone actually reading what I've done – it's so personal and raw - but somehow I believe this is my path to follow.

More soon – my appointment is in fifteen and I'm not out the door yet!

I'm back . . .

It appears that if one does not have a name or a readership, poetry is an unwise choice for either a first-time, no-name poet or a publisher in today's market. The meeting did, however, give me the confidence to keep going. The universal subjects of grief and loss are worthy of pursuing, according to my publisher friend. She suggests I experiment with a different format for the book. Daunting idea, starting again. Recycling it all, really, but I can't stop.

It is clear to me now that when I received all those horrid yet dear family photos this past winter, something deep inside me shifted. New self-rescue plans are forming and I'm letting my heart and head work together to draw up the plans.

Jane

Winter, 2006

Dear Matt,

I'm writing about you – about us and how things have unfolded since your death a little over eight years ago. And though I keep trying to dig into your papers and books to aid my writing process, each time I'm face to face with your things I disintegrate into a sadness that halts me in my tracks. I am determined to write of our journey together since your death, but it seems determination is the only part of a successful equation I have. I stall more often than I move ahead – weeks of no writing compared to only hours at a time with the computer.

Nature and my writing project team to bring me an ugly surprise - a hearty dose of reality. A snow storm buffets the city, closing even the university and forcing my isolation at home. Alone I watch dark skies unload. In times past, I would revel in the gift of unexpected breathing spaces and a snowy walk with your stepfather. Now this extra time could be used for writing, forming and facing the words that re-tell stories of loss. Instead this unexpected event frightens me. I'm alone and lonely.

It disheartens me to realize that without work and its familiar pattern and busyness to keep dark, sad thoughts on hold, I don't trust I have the power to continue to grow any of the new-found courage and hope I started cultivating earlier this year. There is too much thinking space, too much time to re-live too many memories - all highlighted with heavy clouds, quiet hours and a nervous stomach. There's an empty house to keep warm; trees to save from icy wind; deep snow to shovel. There are a myriad of homeowner responsibilities to handle on my own. I sink into self-pity and discover it too late to pretend all is well – to try meditating - to hold my fears at bay.

All this new-found thinking time brings other worries front and center. Your grandmother is frail; since her sister died this past spring, there's a more present sadness in her living. This past summer's fall, when she fractured her pelvis, may well mark the beginning of her end. I'm so far away from her and need to be content with phone calls for decision making and sending love. I realize the nearer Death moves toward her, the more anxious I feel. Time and Death are still formidable enemies even though I know I must find ways to forge friendships with each of them.

I thought the sunshine of summer, the laughter of friends, the joy of being with your sister and your nieces and nephews, the intellectual pastime of reading and analyzing the ideas of others, the joyful work of reinvention, and yes, the anti-depressants, would have given me enough strength to keep the roller coaster nosedives in check. It shocks me that, even having gained so much, there are still times when the knots that tie me to the past and its sorrows can tighten seemingly at will. No control, No control, No control – so hard to accept!

As before I share these thoughts with just you, Matt, because I don't want to with anyone else. I'm sorry that I can't yet keep those earlier promises I made to you; I still believe, more often than not, my pretense of strength is what best keeps me upright. Hopelessness won today. At least now I am able to also anticipate a tomorrow. I am holding on with both hands to Anne Lamott's words in <u>Traveling Mercies</u>: "When you make friends with fear, it can't rule you."

Mom

Faith is the bird that lifts its voice in song while it is yet dark, knowing that the dawn is coming.

Japanese proverb

Part Four: Resurrection

February, 2007 – September, 2008

To love another is to see the face of God
Victor Hugo

Resurrection

Hope is breath,
now lodged, poised and willing, in the soul.

Living arrangements with irretrievable loss
completed,
it sighs, stretching,
finding itself
reaching to liberate possibilities
long held dark.

Destiny shifts.
With a turn, perspective's kaleidoscope
colors its way toward
light.

Soul,
stirring, shifting,
provoking spirit's flow back into newly freed
hands, feet, heart and head,
welcomes pain's exquisite release;
Resurrecting.

Opening to the kiss of Life
while still,
tenderly,
tracing the familiar mask of Death.

"Why is everyone here so happy except me?
'Because they have learned to see goodness and beauty
everywhere, said the Master.'
Why don't I see goodness and beauty everywhere?
'Because you cannot see outside of you what
you fail to see inside.'"
A. deMello, <u>One Minute Wisdom</u>

February, 2007

Misery is a bully – the kind of tyrant that relishes absolute rule. For years now, Grace, I have searched for help to move around it. To trust in goodness, to believe in hope, to feel whole, physically, emotionally and spiritually, has been a dogged quest. Einstein asserted that nothing changes until something moves and I realize I've come to the point of living that truism. Like Gulliver, I am awakening to the fact that I am the help I need - to move through rather than around my own particular bully. I sense something powerful taking shape. New-found strength gathers itself, uttering noises about arranging a resurrection.

I hope you can hear in my words that a shift in my thinking is finally taking root. 2006 was a year of intense and compelling shifts. The roller coaster traveled to highs and lows at mind-numbing speed, causing me more than once to question my own strength –my ability to even hold on for the ride. Still, here I am. I'm making time to meditate and consider faith in watchful and new, untried ways – getting up earlier each day to embrace the quiet and hear my own thoughts. This practice brings me to a gentler, but restless place of knowing I deserve more of what my life has to offer and am convinced that *more* is nearer than I ever believed possible.

There is a purpose beyond simple survival: to extricate myself from my past, untying all parts of me from the cycle of loss and unshed anger that has held me close for far too long. When I write next it will be because I am actually freeing myself and want to share the happy details with you, who faithfully shared the years of silence and sadness.

Jane

April 28, 2007
Happy Birthday my son,

Though I still wish discernment had come sooner, I am finally accepting that there is a rhythm and time to life's happenings that can only be influenced when one gives up trying to control those very things. To believe you are close to me now is enough; hope and the beginnings of trust kindly follow.

I've just encountered this wonderful phrase by author Annie Barrows: ". . . (his) stories were the wallpaper of my life." That simple line marks the volumes of what I now understand you've left with me; not because I have reams of story lines, but because your wallpaper is the overlay for the walls of my heart, vivid in the detail of your storytelling -integral, intimate, ever-present. Your gleeful explanation of the five-second rule of pizza making; your thoughtful recounting of the purity of the scientific method; your joy in irony, detailing your own peril on the streets of Portland as you walk unfamiliar streets trying to amass signatures for your latest cause; the light-hearted but worrisome versions of your sister's junior high adventures – all capturing a view of you, the delighted teller, the inventive plasterer, who lives in me.

Happily, without analyzing or pondering, I simply focus on your presence in my heart, to enjoy and be comforted by the tapestry you have indelibly imprinted there. Today I celebrate bringing you into the world. The love you left with me in our shared memories quietly stirs. I believe, as I continue my writing, more will unfold in layered detail. And though I have tears, I trust they will dry more quickly and softly than before.
Mom

June, 2007
Dear Grace,

The roller coaster has slowed to a crawl and now moves mostly at ground level. My longtime associates - grief, loss, rejection and anger - jump aboard less frequently and stay for shorter rides. Loneliness and I are still close companions but its presence is less bulky, so if I shift slightly I can sometimes see beyond. In my last meeting with the therapist, our talk ended with my decision to once again discontinue the anti-depressant. Unless another enormous crisis transforms the context and direction of my life, I won't be using chemical therapy again. Still engaged in the usual reading, thinking and writing; I'm verging on some important personal discoveries and experimenting with them as tools for picking apart those ties that still keep me close enough to recycle memories.

Just lately I saw the 2004 docudrama, "What The Bleep Do We Know!?" It wasn't my idea to see this movie and admit I went begrudgingly. Since I've spent so much time intellectualizing everything, I generally only want fluff in a movie – situations with no thinking necessary. But within the first five minutes I was mesmerized. It joined spirituality with science and left me chewing on many fascinating abstractions. Quantum physics as the backdrop for learning how to love oneself? Not your usual Saturday afternoon entertainment fare, but because my head and heart flew open in the darkness of that theater, I allowed the film to catapult me into uncharted possibilities. I especially resonated with one of the major conclusions: our thoughts determine the quality of our life, or to paraphrase William James, our greatest discovery is that humans can reshape their existence simply by altering their attitudes toward the lives they are living.

I left the theater excited and hopeful. I have enough control to chart the course for my own change? I can grow new thoughts and produce a new path for my own journey? Affirming those ideas jolted the roller coaster, slowing it to a measured crawl. And just then I caught a brief glimmer of an unfettered me, no longer tied to what was lost, but heading toward the freedom to choose other ways to experience life's paths.

I am off to researching these possibilities.

Jane

July, 2007

Dear patient and perceptive friend,

No surprise I'm sure - I attacked my exploration into changing my thoughts with the fervor of a zealot. I know you remember that the educator in me has a passion for understanding how the brain works as we learn; I'm changing course and extending that same passion into how our brains work as we live. I discovered psychologists, new-age writers, and scientists who readily link science to the spiritual using thought as the context for merging the two. I have been sifting through a collection of thought-centered ideas trying to chart a course for myself.

As promised earlier, here's a thumbnail sketch of some of the most salient notions I embraced from my study. Evolve Your Brain, by Dr. J. Dispenza, was my entry text into the science of the brain and thought. According to the author, "the idea that we can change our brain just by thinking has enormous implications for affecting any kind of change in our life." Taking charge of my own thinking and embracing the power to stop life's travel on a roller coaster. What a seductive idea – being effective enough to cause movement in something, somewhere, somehow, sometime! I was hooked.

From there it was a short leap to the connection between thoughts and emotions. Admittedly simplistic, my way of unpacking Dispenza's much more elegant theory goes like this: my thinking causes me to believe and then feel certain ways toward ideas, things, people and happenings; then those feelings, or emotions, ultimately direct my actions. So . . . I jumped on the hateful coaster on my own and even helped tie all these knots!? If that is to be believed, then by backtracking I should be able to undo as well.

In a world where thought is the beginning, the thinker, me, becomes responsible for all endings. All those sad and loss-filled ideas that I've concentrated on have expanded, and over time I've *become* those thoughts. No wonder I'm so sick of it all. I am grief. Luckily, Dispenza assures that with new feelings come new responses and interactions making change possible. It's time for conscious thought shifts into new patterns of thinking and the trust that healthier emotions will fall into place right behind. I've got the idea, now I just need practice to do the work of actually evolving.

Next I went after spirituality. Though there are a myriad of authors who write about faith and the psychology of connecting thought and spirituality, I just happened to pick up Wayne Dyer's work first and it immediately resonated in both my head and heart. In You'll See It When You Believe It, he states, "It is not what is in the world that determines the quality of your life, it is how you choose to process your world in your thoughts." Meditation is considered by every author I have read a virtual must to help gain both self awareness, growth and peace. My meditation practice - being quiet, listening to my own thoughts and concentrating on what I know is possible and want, rather than what I don't have - is becoming a helpful ritual.

Change is grueling work, but trusting in its possibility and sensing freedom keep me going. One of the knots holding me on the coaster that is the chaos of my past is loosening. I have a faint vision of one hand pulling free, gaining its ability to flex and, given time and practice, shift over to begin releasing the other. My dreaming self feels the lift of the newly-freed arm, its hand moves behind my neck to gently hold, then turn my head from side to side. Finally, I'm able to observe and focus in ways not possible for years. One knot down, three to go to free myself for relocation.

Jane

The road to enlightenment is long and difficult, and you should try not to forget snacks and magazines.
Anne Lamott, Traveling Mercies

September, 2007
Grace,

Fall is close and the crispness of this new season energizes and sharpens my resolve. I've been exercising this new thinking regime and do feel stronger, less at the whim of old emotions, but clearly there is more work to do. As I have come to know myself better, I've discovered that though many people are open to sharing their love with me, and though I own a myriad of beautiful, entertaining and necessary things, over time I willingly made very good friends with the idea of scarcity. Meet my next knot to loosen.

My latest reading guided me into studying the concepts of scarcity and its counterpart, abundance. Since our letters began you've heard me describe life in terms of what I lack; you've watched me put energy into the sadness and anger that surrounds what's missing. Continuing to wallow in this place of lack, or scarcity, only ties me to it more strongly. "If we dwell on scarcity we are putting energy into what we do not have, and this continues to be our experience of life." (Dyer, You'll See It When You Believe It) With that notion ringing in my head, I decided to run in the opposite direction, toward abundance.

The kind of abundance I'm talking about is not about accumulating the material. Rather it is a belief system, an internal conviction that operates to influence my choices in all things. Being in abundance is grounded in the belief that, no matter what, there will always be enough; all I have to do is reach out and I will touch or be touched by what I desire or need.

Additionally, genuinely living into this concept means accepting the notion that I can never truly own anything – not time, not things, not people. According to the pundits, within abundance is real freedom. I admit this abstraction is obscure even to me, the philosophical traveler. Such a belief system moves me as far as I've ever been from control and as such it is foreign to me, daunting, really, but intriguing at the same time.

Some days practicing to apply these two new ideas find me working with paper and pencil, sometimes it takes the form of talking to the angels, other times I use meditation or affirmations, and often I just look in the mirror and tell the person looking back to stop taking herself so seriously. Regardless the practice, the goal remains true - freeing myself for a life ahead.

I let my imagination work: I'm on the roller coaster, my one free hand reaches over to loosen the knot around its mate. They get reacquainted, clasping and clapping and I find myself grinning in satisfaction. I'm halfway to freeing myself and so much more seems possible today.
Jane

We have so little faith in the ebb and flow of life, of love, of relationships. We leap at the flow of the tide and resist in terror its ebb. We are afraid it will never return. We insist on permanency, on duration, on continuity; when the only continuity possible, in life as in love, is in growth, in fluidity – in freedom, in the sense that the dancers are free, barely touching as they pass, but partners in the same pattern.
Anne Lindbergh

January, 2008

Grace, now that I've awakened to the notions of evolving my own thoughts for change and trusting in abundance, I'm dreaming again – or maybe I'm finally keying into them. I awoke this morning feeling the still-radiant warmth of sun-drenched sand beneath me. In last night's dream I was fully clothed, lying on white sand during that time right before full sunrise when light and air are soft with promise and the ground beneath comfortably settled. Both forearms rest behind me, elbows dig into the sand and angle me so that I am leaning and looking both up and out. The horizon is gloriously rich in predawn possibilities. I move to reposition myself, planning to stand and check out what's beyond this sitting spot, but I find I'm held to this place, literally. Both ankles are fixed in place, though I can't see how. Bottom line – I'm going nowhere.

My dream puts me in a place both pleasant and peaceful and even though I am unable to move, I'm unafraid. At the same time, Grace, I think this is a dangerous place. It's just satisfying enough to entice me into resting indefinitely, to seduce me into forgetting there is more. I'm tired – tired of the hard work of creation, of re-piecing, of replacing what's been broken. After all, it's a decent view from here: There's just enough freedom to let me view the possibilities looming on the horizon. It would be so easy to just lie back, to leave behind the reality of those two more knots tying me to both past and present, to numb those questions in my heart still aching to be acknowledged, investigated and healed. To do nothing is a choice.

"We leap at the flow of the tide and resist in terror its ebb. We are afraid it will never return. We insist on permanency, on duration, on continuity; when the only continuity possible, in life as in love, is in growth, in fluidity . . ." Anne Lindbergh hits at the core of an issue that has burdened me since Matt's death, one that solidified into almost palpable fear with BC's departure. For two decades I lived the dream: My children would outlive me and my partner would stay true, loving me throughout the ugliest of times. When neither of those expectations came true, panic took their place. I craved permanency and was terrified that the ebb and flow of life would never again let me rest in the arms of anything lasting or enduring. With study, terror has morphed into the comprehension that permanency, like time, is artificial - a construct created by humans to organize and attach. And with that understanding comes the belief that the next knot tying me in place can only loose when I've learned to embrace the fluidity of life, accepting it as freedom and growth rather than cursing it as another damnable change.

Thanks to a tenacious nature and the primal need to be able to stand and walk into an awakening future, I discovered detachment, the polar opposite of my former master, attachment. Dyer in <u>You'll See It when You Believe It </u>describes attachment as "holding on to something, or defining our life purpose in terms of things or persons external to ourselves. We feel we must have it or some of our essential humanity will be lost." Detachment for me, then, is divesting from the *need* to hold tightly to anyone or anything. It is not letting go of the love I feel or the joy I experience in the presence of who and what I love, but it is disconnecting from the craving to control that love and joy, from the quiet but persistent demand that those people and things stay connected, close, and alive. Dyer posits the essence of detachment this way – running your own life at your own pace on the path of your own choosing while not expecting anyone else to be where you are.

How do I even begin to articulate this newest way of thinking and being into the ebb and flow of my own life? How does anyone learn to allow the action of life to flow undirected, to be totally in the moment, to be free from requiring attachments, free from the suffering when those attachments disappear? I think I need a trainer, a spiritual and emotional physical therapist of sorts to guide me into powering through and beyond this need to need. I turn to a teacher my son would have sought. Buddhist writer Thich Nhat Hanh in Living Buddha, Living Christ tells me that with mindfulness comes the strength to transform suffering and immerse in the art of living in beauty. Mindfulness, a basic Buddhist tenant calling me to be present, conscious and aware in each thought, and to relax into every experience without trying to change or control it, *is detachment*. Clinging to the past has limited my freedom to journey forward, keeping me in the repeating cycle of my own suffering.

Though each step into detachment is difficult, I persist in discovering new ways to approach old ideas. I'm listing my top four most useful ideas so far. If you think they can be of help please use them or give them away. What I'm realizing more and more is we – all of us – are in this odyssey together.

- Ownership of anything is impossible; I can only lease and enjoy for a time what comes into my life. All I encounter flows in and out of my experiences and holding tightly to people and possessions only assures that I will suffer as they inevitably wear away, age, move away and disappear.

- Accepting impermanence saves me from desperately clinging to what brings me joy at the moment. The subtle fear of loss that creeps alongside the pleasure of owning has always been able to destroy the serenity of the moment.

- Everything has a beginning and an ending – fully accepting that reality helps to more deeply appreciate Lindberg's thoughts: ". . . the only continuity possible, in life as in love, is in growth, in fluidity – in freedom, in the sense that the dancers are free, barely touching as they pass, but partners in the same pattern."

- Loss is reality, an incontrovertible part of living. Death and loss are neither unexpected nor unnatural; they just are.

Big question Grace: Could all of this most-recent learning mean that if I relax on the coaster rather than doing all in my power to control its speed and trajectory, it will eventually stop on its own? Has my need to control it actually fueled it? I'd love a wise and speedy answer to this question, but now realize that the most authentic answers never come from outside.

The third knot is unraveling as I write. Both hands are free and thanks to their work, one foot is beginning to move unfettered; three-fourths of my moving parts are ready to propel me into the next stage of this life's journey. Still, I'm reluctant to attack the next knot even though the stakes are too high not to forge ahead. Digging around in the bottom muck of the awe-filled and hazardous well of forgiveness is my next task. I need to trust I'm ready to withstand the anger and guilt that most surely will be unearthed as I tackle this last, most challenging knot.

Thank you for keeping me in your thoughts and prayer for I know you do. I'm sending my love.

"Nothing outside of ourselves has the power to bestow happiness or fulfillment on us. What determines the quality of our life is our choice to be fulfilled or not based on how we think, how we view ourselves and our place in the universe."

W. Dyer, You'll See It When You Believe It

February 2008

Dear Matt,

I find that what the pundits say is true for me. All I can control are my reactions, my interactions, my responses to life around me. Only from those interactions will come my own creation of a humane, generous and well-crafted life. I'm making myself learn how to merely observe rather than interpret life. In the most awkward of ways, I am continually reminded that speaking a possibly true thought or a much-desired outcome does not make either true. So I write my observations to you and expect, in the quiet of my soul, I will hear answers and questions to propel me forward into the continual fireworks of reality – a reality I now realize is surrounded by love and moving to the rhythm of a spirit or universal truths far beyond my ability to understand.

Your grandmother continues her journey toward you. It feels to me that she is only marking time while we who revere her gently and lovingly do the same. I long to more ably practice all the learning I've been gathering over these past months – to think in terms of abundance and gratitude even as I detach from how she survives her days and faces her inevitable end. As always, she helps me grasp what life intends, not only through her living, but now her dying.

I love you.

Mom

"I do not at all understand the mystery of grace –
only that it meets us where we are but does not
leave us where it found us."
Anne Lamott

April, 2008

Grace,

My latest aha idea to share: being heavy into the forgiveness puzzle is "like trying to become a marathon runner in middle age; everything inside me either recoiled, as from a hot flame or laughed a little too hysterically." As if on cue, author Anne Lamott provides a reality check, launching me toward the last knot holding me in place. She goes on to remind me that to be able to experience the goodness life has to offer one has to forgive everyone in her life ". . . even, for God's sake, yourself."

For the last several years I've worried with forgiveness like a dog with an old blanket. Tattered and familiar, the demanding thing seems always to be waiting in the center of the room, tempting me to yet another wrestling match, even though I'm sure I'd dragged it out of sight last time. It's complicated, this old, familiar and demanding quality called forgiveness. My readings and meditative practice have slowly become steeped in it and I am finally ready to accept that I can never move ahead without surrendering to its healing power.

It feels like a solid turning point, having this analytical and spiritual discussion with myself about forgiveness. It goes something like this: to travel into healing, I can't only be cognitively involved with the concept but actually must gentle my emotional side into also opening to forgiveness in all of its complexities. And, for clarity, I first have to name and admit to what rests at the very core of my underlying resentments, anger and guilt – what needs forgiving. Their names became abandonment by a husband, failure of a mother, and decisions of a son. The hopeless thoughts and accompanying emotions, the scarcity mentality and the conviction that I could hold tightly to what had already slipped through my fingers, have all been busily defining my life choices - defining me.

I think forgiveness will be my game changer. My study of it reports that when one forgives another it is a way of cutting off the power of that *other*, outside ourselves, to control our thoughts and behaviors. Forgiveness is the means to free us for a future untainted by old wounds - easy to verbalize, really tough to actually accomplish.

As you know my work forgiving BC has been a disjointed proposition. Feelings of abandonment and resentment surrounding his leaving our relationship were so tightly wrapped together with Matt's loss that I put them on hold for years. My forgiveness for BC's part in my pain is relatively fresh. I think it's a safe conjecture that had I a partner by my side who was able to love me unconditionally during those most awful and dangerous years I would have experienced a different grief journey – one more gentle and hopeful than the one I lived alone. But that was not to be my reality.

Finally becoming healthy enough to admit aloud how being on my own without a loving partner altered both me and my entire grief journey, catapults into the light all my underlying abandonment issues, placing them squarely in my sight line. Thankfully, I've come to know that muddling through each unhappy, unhealthy decision is no longer worth the analyzing time it takes. Instead, I return to what I've been practicing – to detach from the need to hold tightly to what has past – declaring that enough time has been spent dwelling on a disintegrated relationship. My forgiveness, letting in light to dispel the long-held thoughts and emotions tied to personal rejection and disillusionment, dismantles their power and allows for the burial of something long dead.

Forgiveness of another, I find, is far easier than forgiving myself. Self-discovery through therapy, reading, discussion and meditation help me realize I expect more strength and understanding, more love and thoughtfulness from myself than anyone else. I give others a pass when it comes to being their best selves no matter the situation. Whether right or wrong, that has been my style; consequently, self reproach is generally center stage. For me to love myself into a better future, it's paramount that I grow beyond these operating patterns. I believe it is forgiveness that can open the door to my new beginnings.

The time I give to considering Matt's final years and our disconnected relationship is leading me to a peace I haven't felt before. I am acknowledging his right to live in ways only he could have understood and directed. Little by little I am disentangling my heart and head from the blame and depression that so effortlessly triggers self-loathing when I think of what my son and I did not have time to experience. Forgiveness for both of us is finding root. In quiet, he and I work toward this together.

So there it is, Grace. The final knot falls open. In theory I'm free from the tangle of pain that has held me in place for so long. The plan is to rest some, look around and stretch my arms and legs as the coaster, as if by a master plan, comes to a final stop. Climbing out could be tricky so I'll approach that carefully; I'm stiff and tired, even a little dizzy. Traveling for years in maze-like circles can do that to you.

This journey is winding down, dear friend. The hardest work may be over for now, but I don't plan to be without you. More soon -
Jane

April, 2008
My son,

Since I've been meditating on forgiveness it has become clear to me that I have been quietly and guiltily disappointed, confused, even angry with you for a while now. Unable to admit it even to myself until now, I hope acknowledging these most real emotions will somehow free me to become more honest with myself. Those last years when you may have thought of me but kept me far away from your life felt like a ruthless condemnation of me and our relationship. Even though I continued to try to maintain contact through packages, intermittent calls, and holiday gifts, those two years with no word from you - not at Christmas, birthdays, Mother's Days, or even to announce your long-awaited university graduation day - made it clear you had made a choice to be free of me.

I tried repeatedly to understand, to put myself in your place – a young man who intentionally broke free from established family expectations, who was continually learning how to operate within the fluctuating boundaries and chronic pain of a disease that had already robbed you of so many physical activities. You purposefully established a lifestyle on your own with friends who took for granted those things that I, your mom, might only see as painful changes. I believed you knew you were cutting me out of your life and, though at times the edges of my agonizing hurt and anxiety were laced with hot flashes of anger, I always took on the estrangement as my fault. I have lived with the belief that I must have done or not done something to have earned your silence. That time in limbo is hell defined.

It is time to clear the air and name my feelings so I can move on. I've got to come to terms with the feelings of rejection and flashes of anger that keep my spirit flat on its back. You were so bright and, I thought, wise. Your seeming acceptance of and adaptation to the Ankylosing Spondilitis and its consequences, your quick smile and ability to forge friendships, as well as your love of and investment in ideas and philosophies, made you a prime candidate for a rich, involved, interesting life. I thought you were establishing just that so I waited as you settled into your new job at the university library, with your new car and new degree. I was giving the newly-graduated you time to realize that even after two years I was still only a phone call, a quick note, a whispered prayer away from you. My arms were always open. I cried; I prayed and sought guidance; I sent my unconditional love across the miles daily. And you died.

My question this time is not if you knew I loved you unconditionally through it all, but how much did you love and express that love to yourself? Were those last scholarly years a gentle way to keep from participating in a life beyond its erudite isolation? Did your mindful, day-to-day living make future planning unnecessary? Were you simply unaware of the physical clues your earthly body provided - too used to consistent pain to notice? Really, my brilliant boy, how often did you wonder if those over-the-counter pain killers you were taking might be as harmful as they were helpful? Did you accept the possibility of that ulcer, continually-eroding, poised for disaster? Did you plan to build an "us" again sometime – after something?

I've wrestled with these questions for years and finally believe I have lived into some answers that ring true for me: Your existence depended on the shifting sand of how well you felt each day. Instead of planning ahead, thinking about your future health, you learned to claim each individual day as your own personal gift, living each your way - fully - no matter the cost to an uncertain tomorrow. Your only plan: finding some joy, some gladness, a measure of personal fulfillment in each of those days. The future would be taking care of itself. Am I close?

To forgive us both is my practice now: You, because you created and accepted a life that operated without your mom; me, because I remained powerless - unaware of your slide into an early death. Forgive is an active verb. To live it requires me to push forward. I'm moving into my newest understanding, a fresh truth I'm struggling to internalize: You were free to make all decisions pertaining to your own living. Your actions were about and for you, not me. This very freedom of choice is the basis of our humanity, mine and yours. My job as your mom is not to continue wondering, explaining or blaming. I only need to relax into the flow of what is real – in life you were beautiful and loving; now you are gone, but even in death you urge me to note beauty, continue in love and develop wisdom. Detachment and acceptance, even during this month that marks another year's birthday that will go uncelebrated, are slowly but certainly propelling me beyond the need to name, control or untangle your choices the last years of your life.

I love you. I am proud of you - then, now, forever -

Mom

August, 2008

My dear Grace,

Just a small note to say thank you. Yes, the flowers are from me. I'm so glad you like them. I thought I remembered you, like my boy, love sunflowers. Such an audacious-looking plant, the sunflower. I'm reminded of the tenacity of life when I catch sight of their bold, rich-green stalks and brash, colorful flower. They are a simple token of my gratefulness to you, my generous confidante. I know I've thanked you throughout the years, but I'm realizing I can never say it enough. Do you know how instrumental you have been in changing, really saving, my life? Your faithfulness to my journey and unconditional regard for both my pain and joy during the past decade have helped to deposit me in a new and healthier space. More than listener, more than friend, you, my generous and compassionate teacher, have helped guide me into the embrace of that life-affirming blessing - Grace. I expect you will be with me forever. How lucky am I, dear friend?

Jane

Grace is the central invitation to life, and the final word.
It's the beckoning nudge and the overwhelming,
undeserved mercy which urges us to change and grow,
and then gives us the power to pull it off.
Tim Hansel, <u>You Gotta Keep Dancin'</u>

September, 2008

My dear son,

My time thinking about the place soul, spirit and grace have in my life has morphed and grown in complexity over this tempestuous journey since your death ten years ago this month. I'm no longer angry at God. Though I still admit to confusion about how your death fits as a piece in the puzzle that is religion, God no longer gets blamed for your death - or for me outliving my child. I believe you and God met along the way and had come to terms together; my concerns or anger really no longer apply. When I began this odyssey, hope was a few boards nailed to a house named grief. Now that metaphor is reversed; hope is my home, and grief, assorted boards that sometime arrange patterns on its surface. I am grateful.

As Grandma grows closer and closer to your world I draw more into residing in hope. My greatest wish is that she is resting in deep peace, in an assurance of grace in each moment. As she transitions to encounter you may she easily find the kind of grace Christian ethicist Lewis Smedes describes in <u>The Art of Forgiving</u>: ". . . the gift of feeling sure that our future, even our dying is going to turn out more splendidly than we dare imagine." It is weight lifted to accept fully the notion that the when, where, and how of her death is beyond my ability to predict or control. And though I may be privileged to hold her hand in this life, it's you, my son, who will throw the welcome-home party.

I have had a decade to learn from your loss: a decade of searching and readjusting, of crafting one and yet another, newer version of a life journey, of crying when your sweet face comes to me unbidden, and smiling when that same vision is wrapped in hope and expectation.

Ego's best friend, control, has been a frightful enemy and breaking free from its powerful authority continues my ongoing battle. Talking with you has given me tools for the fight. When it comes to control, I have learned the necessity of observing and processing the unfolding of things before I intervene, rather than expecting I have the power to readily interpret and direct life. I've been served with consistent reminders that speaking a partially-understood thought or a much-loved outcome will not automatically make either true. Wishing most definitely does not make it so.

Asking you questions granted me the wisdom to understand that dwelling in the quiet of my own soul, available to hear answers as well as generate new questions, can empower me to most safely and productively propel into the fireworks of reality – a reality surrounded by possibilities and moving to a rhythm independent of my control. You've been an exceptional teacher my son.

You continue to be in my life, my waking dreams, my best hopes, my best self. How much and strongly I love you continues to feed me. I feel your arm around my shoulders, your infectious grin is a presence just over my right shoulder and I believe if I turn my head ever so slightly I can be lost in its loving light. I don't know what is next for us, but I do know that our isolation has ended.

You are always my boy, always with me, and I am ever your grateful Mom.

Addendum for Grace

2008

. . . just talk about what you think is saving your life now: this statement brought my reading to an abrupt halt. Barbara Brown Taylor's words in An Altar in the World immediately ping-ponged around my brain, resting briefly on one idea, then another thought and then another. What is saving my life? And with that question I tumble back into the past.

I name my Saviors and note that they have changed over time. When Matt died, I counted on those who proved they knew how to unconditionally love me to save me, to keep me alive, to help me open my eyes to tomorrows. When BC left me, I fell into the intellectual arms of strangers and colleagues whose words, ideas, and experiences taught me ways to honor and salvage remnants of a lifestyle slowly disintegrating. In time I worked to save myself by using skills and new understandings to make decisions and alter the way I thought about and lived life. Saviors change. And, luckily for us all, saviors abound.

My ten-year travel brought me many saviors, not all to whom I listened well, but many were in the right time, the right place with the right words I needed to hear. So many redeeming gifts were showered on me by philosophers and friends, authors, poets, artists and family. I decided to collect a top ten list of those ideas that were life-savers for me, gathered from ten years of carrying around a heart that was learning the pattern of stitches to mend itself.

10. Understand that a bereaved couple can't bear the pain of the death of a child equally or, perhaps even similarly. They become singles, mourning individually as separate grieving humans. Death of a child trumps any grief experienced earlier.

9. Accept that you might be sensitive to how you appear - emotionally, spiritually or even physically - to family, friends, colleagues and acquaintances. Even though you wear the disguises of a coping self, you will long for them to remember that grief has no appropriate timelines, no fixed face, and you are ever and always a grieving parent.

8. Treat yourself as if you are your own child, your own best friend, and follow your best advice to him/her; immerse yourself in the emotional, spiritual and physical support and self-care you would want for someone you love.

7. Do not sit in judgment of your emotions, no matter how erratic they become. They are simply what they are – neither good nor bad.

6. Be open to a loving support system, a safe place where you can be honest and share thoughts no matter how ugly they may seem. Say out loud your outrage and anxieties. Learn the symptoms, rules and processes of grief to reduce the fear of losing yourself in its maelstrom.

5. Hold on to the beauty of the possible - even in the blackest end of despair. There will be better times; you will genuinely laugh again, and your grief will learn to play a different, less pain-filled role when you make room for the light of hope into your days and nights.

4 Stop trying to order or stringently plan for a life of the familiar; it flows outside your control. Practice becoming aware of all that is present around you and live into the beauty of those things one day at a time.

3. Accept that the pain you feel cannot be circumvented. Grief, in its many iterations, must be experienced in order to move through it into a place of healing.

2. Establish a daily practice of bringing grace to the inner you. Use prayer, meditation, talking to the angels or whatever else brings quiet, deep comfort.

1. Realize that the most important question in life will never be answered to your satisfaction: *Why did my child die?* There is no acceptable answer. There is only putting one foot in front of the other to walk into a new reality.

Saviors are everywhere. Search for them with as clear a focus as you can muster. Rest in their loving advice and believe them when they say *you are loved.* Uncover the savior that lives inside you; listen and take to heart all the grace-filled messages preparing you for the possible and reminding you to love yourself. Don't be afraid of the space in between what has been and what can be: Simply spend a quiet moment to wrap and warm yourself within your own arms . . . then step forward. There's a door just ahead, opening into the light of a new time.

"Don't cry because it's over.
Smile because it happened."
Dr. Seuss